Product, Platform and Audience

AN EXECUTIVE-LEVEL GUIDE TO
BUILDING SCALABLE CONTENT-BASED
B2B MEMBERSHIP BUSINESSES

Robert J Phillips

Emerging Technology Networks
MELBOURNE, AUSTRALIA

Emerging Technology Networks
P.O. Box 362, 440 Collins Street,
Melbourne, Victoria, 3000, Australia
www.emergingtechnologynetworks.com

Ordering Information:
Quantity sales. Special discounts are available on quantity purchases by corporations, associations, and others. For further information please contact the "Sales Department" at the address above.

Product, Platform and Audience / Robert J Phillips. —1st edition
ISBN 978-0-6482775-0-7

Disclaimer

The material in this publication is of the nature of general comment only, and does not represent professional advice. It is not intended to provide specific guidance for particular circumstances and it should not be relied on as the basis for any decision to take action or not take action on any matter which it covers.

Readers should obtain professional advice where appropriate, before making any such decision. To the maximum extent permitted by law, the author and publisher disclaim all responsibility and liability to any person, arising directly or indirectly from any person taking or not taking action based on the information in this publication.

Table of contents

For my wife and family…

> *"Audiences are shifting. Platforms are shifting. Ages are shifting. It's better to be in charge of change than to have to react to change."*

—Roger Ailes

> *"Content is King."*

—Bill Gates

> *"Because the internet is so new, we still don't really understand what it is."*

—Douglas Adams

> *"Everything I publish is for my readers."*

—Felix Dennis

CHAPTER 1

Background

A t its core, this is a book about change and progression within the global publishing industry; and how to innovate in terms of both technology and methodology in order to create and then maximise opportunities to exploit these changes.

The fundamental changes the publishing sector has experienced since the mid 1990's have proven extraordinary for established businesses operating within the sector.

Some would argue that change started before the digital revolution, with the Wapping dispute in Great Britain in 1986, where archaic business practices and a heavily unionised industry was forced to come to terms with technological change and embrace new printing technologies.

However, if you concentrate solely upon the changes to the industry that have occurred since the advent of the World Wide Web, then you are talking about fundamental, revolutionary change. Change not just to the methodologies of the production and consumption of content, but to the entire competitive landscape and ecosystem that publishing businesses operate within.

As a 40-something who has spent his entire career operating within the digital medium, I have experienced many of the seismic changes first hand. I have been both on the front lines dealing with digital transformations and also, for the past 15+ years the business decision maker attempting to navigate and prognosticate the future direction of an industry I love.

Career-wise, it's fair to describe myself as a digital native.

My journey starts off at University in the mid-1990's by building one of Britain's first e-commerce-enabled web platforms for the family business. Here, I quickly learnt what works and (perhaps just as importantly) what does not work when developing an e-commerce business able to compete in the space.

I went from specialising in building e-commerce platforms... to building white label affiliate solutions... to building digital audiences to support those properties... and then on to sales, be they $100 or $1 million subscriptions to membership-based properties, or advertising and marketing services portals.

Today, I have amassed 15+ years proven leadership experience at CEO and Executive-level.

Through a comprehensive understanding of (1) product; (2) proposition; and (3) potential opportunity, I have gained a reputation for strategic vision, innovation, audience hyper-growth and achieving outstanding financial results.

I am immensely proud that the digital businesses and/or products envisaged, created and then managed have combined generated in excess of $130 million in profit, with exceptional margins for a variety of large >$1.5 Billion media conglomerates listed on the LSE through to exciting start-up, or early-stage companies in the UK, the US and Australia.

We've got a long journey ahead of us in this book as we investigate exciting new opportunities, technologies and methodologies. Let's get started!

Key Assumptions

Below is a brief list of the assumptions I have used when putting this document together:

FUNDING – The business has at least $2 million (AUD) in capital available to it.

VALUE TO THE ENTERPRISE – You are looking to create a business, or add value to an existing enterprise by launching a new membership portal.

POSITIVITY AND IMAGINATION – It should go without that you need to have a team that is positive, imaginative, dedicated and want to achieve success together.

STAFF – You can source staff, be they technical, editorial, or marketing as per requirements.

INDUSTRY SENTIMENT – The industry is ready and the core products are still marketable.

OFFSHORE PRODUCTION – You are open to sourcing some content and/or web development activity offshore.

UNDERSTANDING – You have a professional-level understanding of the digital economy.

CHAPTER 2

Introduction

A couple of things you will immediately notice about this book are (1) my writing style; and (2) the format. I make no apology for writing this book using my style and voice, which I would best describe as 'no nonsense'.

The book has been written in a way to best offer insight and ideas to drive tangible innovation for senior executives either already operating within, or looking to operate within the sector.

In terms of the format of the book, it is structured somewhat differently to most with the aim of enabling the Executive, or entrepreneur to efficiently find the information they require and garner the required understanding from it.

Many of the ideas expressed within the book have symbiotic, or synergistic relationships with the other concepts. I have attempted to keep the relationships between the relevant ideas as clear as possible.

In order to demonstrate the ideas and concepts the book outlines a fictional platform business, operating across a select number of emerging technology verticals.

It is likely that the sectors you will be looking to service with your real business will be different from these. This should not matter too much though as the methods and ideas are easily transferable. This book has been written so as to be as relevant to entrepreneurs and senior executives looking at launching a portal covering automotive, financial services, logistics, or pretty much any other notable vertical as it is to the emerging technology space.

Business Overview

This fictional business is a network of subscription-based premium industry intelligence portals, or 'vortals' as I sometimes call them. Powered by artificial intelligence and proprietary data, each individual portal services high-value global emerging technology verticals, ranging from genomics and alternative energy through to space technology and virtual reality.

The business features products and functionality that will be both revolutionary for the business of content; and massively scalable into just about any industry vertical (or horizontal).

This business operates within the membership economy and additionally sells premium R&A reports, advertising solutions and marketing services.

Competitive Intelligence

The SWOT Analysis of the company offers a focussed, neutral insight into our example portal business and its positioning within the greater digital media landscape.

STRENGTHS

MANAGEMENT – The business is led by an elite team with great R&A and digital media experience.

NEW TECHNOLOGY – The business will have developed new platform technology that will enable the business to rapidly replicate its properties into new verticals.

GROWTH INDUSTRIES – The business is concentrated on high growth industry verticals, both in terms of employees and revenue potential.

SUBSCRIPTIONS – The business will lock many of its customers into 1 or 2 year subscriptions.

GLOBAL IN REACH – The business is global in emphasis and reach and therefore not bound by local economies.

WEAKNESSES

RESOURCES – The business is capital and resource constrained.

LOCATION – The business needs to establish a physical presence and sales office in other key territories to maximise future growth.

CONTENT CREATION – Content creation and editorial is a large cost for the business.

CLIENT INTERACTION – Growth at the business requires regular client interaction with advertisers, subscribers and facilitators.

OPPORTUNITIES

TECHNOLOGICAL ADVANCEMENT – Recent and ongoing developments in the field of machine learning has enabling the core product to be produced.

INDUSTRY GROWTH – To use the technology infrastructure, methodologies and capabilities to enter attractive new industry sectors.

CONTENT – To reduce the cost of content production, whilst maintaining the quality and uniqueness of the content offering.

SCALABILITY – To improve the scale and gain efficiencies in IT development and utilisation.

BUILD RELATIONSHIPS – To use established key business relationships in new markets.

THREATS

NEW COMPETITOR – To not access as many new verticals as possible, thus allowing a competitor to emerge and compete for market share (lose market dominance).

TECHNOLOGY FAILURE – For the products or brand to be compromised either accidentally or overtly.

CAPITAL – To lack the capital to convert current opportunities into revenue.

EXPANSION RISKS – New vertical and regional expansion adds to risk and costs.

The Target Markets

The global B2B media and information industry is growing. Revenue in 2016 alone was estimated to be $28.35 Billion (USD).

Combined the industry verticals I have concentrated on within this book, it currently equates to an approximate market size of $1.6 Trillion (USD). Combined, the industries are predicted to grow to approximately $3 Trillion (USD) by the early 2020's and are likely to continue growth into the following decades.

Global in reach, the business is at its core a series of templated industry vertical portals covering the following defined industry sectors:

VIRTUAL AND AUGMENTED REALITY

Total revenue for virtual reality (VR) and augmented reality (AR) is projected to increase from $5.2 billion in 2016 to over $162 billion in 2020, according to research vendor IDC.

SPACE TECHNOLOGY

The space economy is stated to be worth in excess of $325 Billion (USD) in 2017, with accelerated industry growth over the next century.

ARTIFICIAL INTELLIGENCE

It is estimated that revenue generated from the direct and indirect application of AI software will grow from $1.4 billion in 2016 to $59.8 billion by 2025.

ALTERNATIVE AND RENEWABLE ENERGY

Even the most conservative estimates put the global clean energy market as topping $1.35 Trillion in 2016. With much geopolitical will and new technological breakthroughs this will be a high growth sector for decades to come.

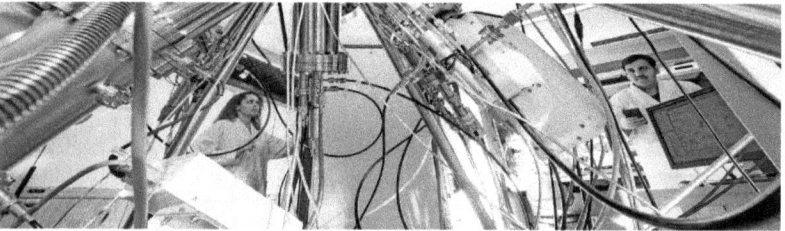

BIOINFORMATICS AND GENOMICS

The global bioinformatics market generated $4.80bn in 2015. The research vendor VisionGain forecasts the overall world bioinformatics market will achieve revenue of $11.43 Billion (USD) by 2020.

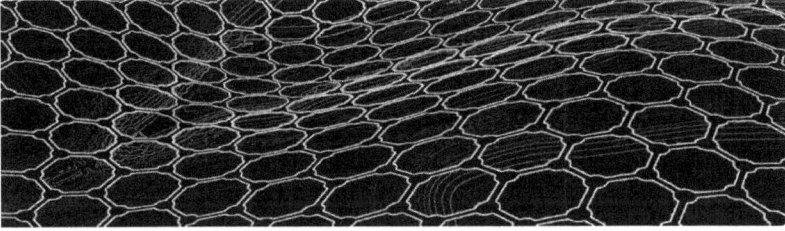

NANOTECHNOLOGY

The global nanotechnology market should reach $90 Billion (USD) by 2021 from $39 Billion (USD) back in the year 2016. This equates to a compound annual growth rate of 18.2 per cent.

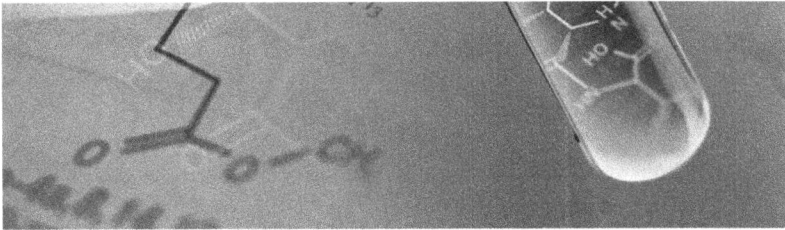

PHARMACEUTICAL TECHNOLOGY

The global pharmaceutical technology sector consists of a number of niche industries, including medical technology and biotechnology.

According to the R&A vendor Statista, the current market size of the medical technology sector is $403 Billion, rising to in excess of $500 Billion by 2022.

Add in the biotechnology sector, which is currently estimated to be have a market size of $140 Billion, then it is fair to guesstimate that the combined market size will top $750 Billion by the mid 2020's.

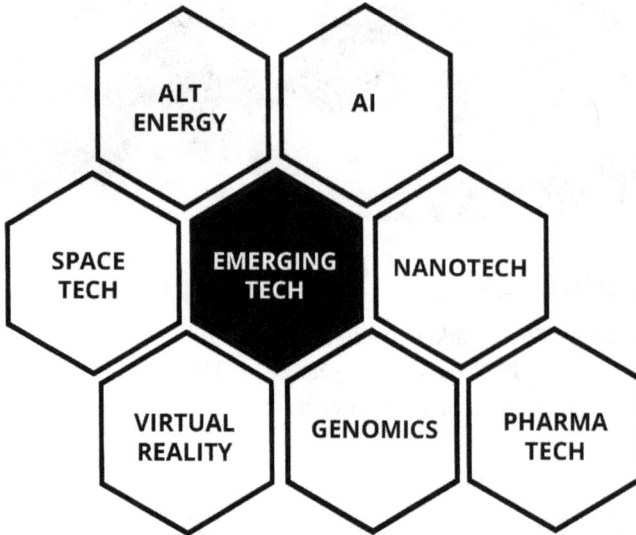

Global in outlook, each individual portal is designed to be *the* industry-leading source of news, knowledge and information for professionals working within the defined sector.

To meet changing usage patterns; and to ensure greater usability of the proprietary interface, each portal will be designed to be accessible via modern internet browsers and via phone and tablet-based Android and iOS apps utilising both voice initiated and visual navigation.

Strategy

T his section of the book outlines a medium-term corporate strategy for our example business, along with operational strategies to ensure the health and progression of the company and its products.

Corporate Strategy

It is vitally important to start the business off on the right foot. This means positioning.

In terms of enterprise valuations, a huge issue for any new business within the publishing space will be that it is deemed an editorial-driven company.

It is widely acknowledged by investors that editorial-based businesses are marginal and barely break-even, if at all. The cost of producing the product is simply too high and not scalable enough. This single issue results in 1-4x margin-based valuations rather than a valuation that is 4-8x revenue.

To help alleviate this, the fictional business will develop a proprietary job board. This will potentially change the narrative from low margin publishing to scalable 'classifieds' platform. Classifieds-based businesses achieve a valuation from a potential 6-12x revenue multiple.

Also, to help alleviate the 'publishing' categorisation issue one plausible strategy could be to secondarily pivot to a SaaS model.

You could achieve a valuation of 4-8x SDE, which in this case would equate to a similar number to 4-8x EBITDA. Not at the level of a classifieds business, but still higher than traditional publishers.

Additionally, it will be worth looking at small, niche acquisitions in the $20-80k range, preferably website that are barely (if at all) monetised. These would add quite a lot of usage to the business; and open up potential new angles. Synergy on low-cost acquisitions include:

- → Relevant industry, or interest area
- → Relevant demographic, or country
- → Relevant content
- → Relevant functionality

Key Success Factors

If you look at the key factors that potentially dictate success, or failure for businesses operating in the digital publishing space, you can then gauge what you need to do in order to increase the odds for success.

Whilst each of the following points are self-explanatory and will be visited systematically throughout the document, I have also included a brief description of them below in order to set a guide for the project:

USER FRIENDLY – The platform and all usage-based products should be well designed, easy to use, learn and offer the correct functional specification accessible to the market.

ACCESS TO SKILLED STAFF – Industry operators require a skilled workforce both in terms of platform development and content production. This ensures that the product is available to the market.

IP AND COPYRIGHT PROTECTIONS – A business relying on revenue from a subscription-based product must protect its core IP to ensure that the product and/or content cannot be accessed for free elsewhere.

VALUE – Any business publishing on the internet should provide significant value to its end user in terms of quality, variation, timeliness and cost effectiveness.

TARGET AND FOCUS – A membership platform aimed at professionals working within niche industry verticals should only target those relevant to the business.

Corporate Philanthropy

Strategically, it would be wise for any industry membership business to outline to its users its inherent belief in and support of the industry it serves. This is a theme I will return to later in the book. For now though, one way in which it could be seen as having these values is through corporate philanthropy.

For example, Education and access to technology have been identified as key drivers to achieving a fairer playing field for future generations.

Therefore, each year the parent company would aim to give away 10 per cent of its net profit to registered charities in the education space, as democratically voted for by its shareholders at the AGM, or by its membership.

This is a key statement that could be made on the website and to members. It would go down exceptionally well with the users of the product and centre the business as being a platform supporting the industry and society as a whole.

A supplementary by-product of a policy in this area could be a positive impact the membership churn rate both for individual subscribers and for corporate members.

Customer Driven Strategy

The fast pace of change within the internet economy reinforces the need for continual and progressive innovation in order to prosper. The business outlined in this book will therefore develop strategies that adapt to the changing nature of both the internet economy and changes to the relevant emerging tech sectors.

Part of this progressive approach towards product development will entail (1) embracing new usage patterns and content types, such as video; (2) integrations with new and developing technologies, such as Google AI job search; and (3) adapting to the problems experienced by forever changing and evolving industry landscape.

Operational Strategy

The business will need to implement best practices across personnel, recruitment, work processes and company procedures in order to ensure legal compliance, staff training and talent retention.

In addition to these, the business will aim to create and maintain the technology platform, an optimal sales funnel for its commercial offerings and best in class content, which will support membership retention efforts and the perceived value of the membership propositions.

Core Competencies

By identifying a select number of core competencies, the business can develop the best processes such as customer satisfaction, product development and professional relationships with stakeholders.

The core competencies of our example business are:

➜ **PROVIDING OF DIGITAL PRODUCT AND SERVICES TO SUBSCRIBERS**

➜ **PROVIDING A SUPERIOR TECHNOLOGY PLATFORM TO ACT AS A PORTAL FOR THE INDUSTRY**

➜ **PROVIDING SOLUTIONS CAREER-RELATED PROBLEMS TO PROFESSIONALS**

➜ **PROVIDING A SUPERIOR STANDARD OF CUSTOMER AND CLIENT SATISFACTION**

➜ **PROVIDING MARKETING SOLUTIONS TO BUSINESSES REQUIRING ACCESS TO OUR AUDIENCE**

Defining the Culture and Values

With the business both operating within emerging portions of the global economy I believe the business needs to ultimately define a set of values, which in-turn develop into a corporate culture.

These values and this culture should be noted in the employee handbook for reference.

Corporate Values

Below are the seven core values that I believe are relevant for this kind of dot-com publishing business.

1. **VALUE** – We seek to offer value to our members and customers by helping them solve the problems and challenges they face.

2. **RELATIONSHIPS** – We understand that our business is built around the building and maintaining of relationships.

3. **EXCELLENCE** – We aspire to be the very best at everything we do; and we learn from our mistakes.

4. **LEADERSHIP** – We pride ourselves on our leadership within the spaces we operate.

5. **TEAMWORK** – We are passionate about collaboration and engagement.

6. **COURAGE** – We are entrepreneurial, we create tangible innovations and thus take risks.

7. **SPEED** – We operate at speed.

Remember, the values of the business both exist within; and define its overall culture.

Corporate Culture

It is my firm belief that a culture of a business equates to the collective personality of the organisation. Its culture is not just who we are as a company, but what we as a collective truly aspire to be.

For any business operating in multiple locales, potentially located within different States, different countries, maybe in radically different time zones the corporate culture is the *one big thing* will bind the business together.

Team Make-up

One of the factors in success in the creative industry such as digital publishing is the hiring of the right type of people. You can massively improve the odds on you succeeding if you hire the right kind of people.

Certainly, you do not want to start off on the wrong foot and then attempt to grow a company where the staff consists of disruptive influences, Social Justice Warriors, or what I like to call 'Woke' political activists.

Instead, you want a company with likeminded, pro-active and positive collaborators, hopefully with a deep interest in the vertical, or interest-area covered. In the example business we use in this book the industries are emerging technology verticals.

Many publishing businesses make poor recruitment decisions. Hires that from my experience increase the potential for discourse, activism, conflict and unnecessary unionisation. Fairfax is an example of one such a business.

This can cause massive disruption, PR disasters and even be a business killer.

The fundamental issue stems from two main factors, (1) a broken business model for the publishing sector; and (2) high wage economies across the Anglosphere. Combined these significant factors create a degree of pessimism and a touch of paranoia, especially when the industry they are covering is rightly deemed financially poor, overly reliant upon the public purse, or in decline.

Moving-forward, to counter these problems I would suggest that online publishers move to a gig-based collaboration model, where you focus on talent, individual tasks and paying for contributions.

Many businesses already operating within the information economy would likely save more than the additional spend outlined in this book purely by moving to this model, especially if some of the tasks and contributions were from overseas.

Remember, with the digitalisation of the global economy, the entirety of the English-speaking world is at the business owners disposal.

Those permanent staff the business requires will have a strong digital-focused skillset, a track record of tangible achievements, along with great attitude and experience and/or network within the chosen sector. These factors are more important to success, however an understanding of the verticals is also absolutely key.

The Financial Model

In this section of the book I will outline the core principals behind modelling a business from a financial and operations perspective.

The type of modelling I prefer is less based around 'grand thinking' and more towards known costings, industry average performances and if at all possible actuals.

The model normally is normally three years, although if I have a specific milestones for capital raising in mind I may increase this to five years.

After the model has been completed the variables included can be amended to forecast and predict future performance.

Additionally, the beauty of the model is that it can easy be transformed into a P&L and management report.

Outline of the Model

For the example portal business used in this book, the model will consist of the following 12 pages:

1. RESULTS PAGE
2. MONTHLY TRAVEL
3. INDIVIDUAL SUBSCRIPTIONS MODEL
4. CORPORATE SUBSCRIPTIONS MODEL
5. REPORT SALES
6. ADVERTISING SALES
7. MARKETING PLAN
8. CONTRIBUTOR PAYMENT MODEL
9. HR COSTS
10. ASSORTED COSTS
11. BUDGET DETAIL
12. CONTENT MATRIX

Now we have the structure for the model, let us build the model. For this I use Excel and logic.

Building it

This section outlines the attributes and methodology of each portion of the model used for the example business.

RESULTS PAGE

The results page operates as an overview of the business broken down by year. As a result, it is on this page that the annual totals for each of the individual pages are brought together and added up.

The attributes included on this page are as follows:

- ➜ INDIVIDUAL SUBSCRIPTIONS – BY YEAR
- ➜ CORPORATE SUBSCRIPTIONS – BY YEAR
- ➜ REPORT SALES – BY YEAR
- ➜ BANNER SALES – BY YEAR

➔ STOREFRONT SALES – BY YEAR
➔ LICENSING / PARTNERSHIPS – BY YEAR
➔ R&D GRANT – BY YEAR
➔ TOTAL REVENUE – BY YEAR
➔ EBIT $ – BY YEAR
➔ EBIT % – BY YEAR
➔ YoY REVENUE GROWTH
➔ YoY OPEX GROWTH
➔ YoY MARGIN GROWTH ($)
➔ YoY MARGIN GROWTH ($)
➔ ENTERPRISE VALUE – BY YEAR BASED ON REVENUE MULTIPLES
➔ ENTERPRISE VALUE – BY YEAR BASED ON EBITDA MULTIPLES

At the bottom of the page, I like to highlight each annual revenue breakdown as a pie chart.

Finally, it is worth building this page after you have completed the other pages.

MODEL RESULTS

GROUP REVENUES	YEAR 1	YEAR 2	YEAR 3	YEAR 4	YEAR 5
INDIVIDUAL SUBSCRIPTIONS	$58,308	$751,205	$2,218,079	$4,091,359	$6,158,982
CORPORATE SUBSCRIPTIONS	$99,334	$882,833	$2,058,258	$3,429,101	$4,675,291
REPORT SALES	$16,850	$79,725	$219,600	$381,400	$537,600
BANNER SALES	$75,862	$153,378	$227,963	$392,015	$752,457
STOREFRONT SALES	$112,544	$776,302	$1,688,516	$2,628,083	$8,797,776
LICENSING / PARTNERSHIPS	$0	$400,000	$400,000	$1,800,000	$2,000,000
R&D GRANT	$250,000	$500,000	$500,000	$500,000	$500,000
TOTAL REVENUE	$612,699	$3,343,443	$7,312,217	$12,421,952	$18,422,106

OPEX	YEAR 1	YEAR 2	YEAR 3	YEAR 4	YEAR 5
MARKETING	$174,908	$259,500	$297,900	$341,100	$589,100
HR COSTS	$1,894,946	$3,758,476	$4,212,709	$4,772,900	$5,489,752
OFFICE AND ADMINISTRATION	$432,450	$355,100	$362,000	$479,100	$429,900
FINANCE AND PROFESSIONAL SERVIC	$46,100	$45,900	$45,900	$45,900	$45,900
DIRECTORS FEES	$37,500	$75,000	$75,000	$75,000	$75,000
TOTAL OPEX	$2,585,904	$4,493,976	$4,993,509	$5,714,000	$6,367,652

PROFITABILITY	YEAR 1	YEAR 2	YEAR
EBIT ($)	-$1,973,205	-$1,150,533	$2,318,7
EBIT (%)	-322%	-34%	32%

YoY GROWTH	YEAR 1	YEAR 2	YEAR
REVENUE GROWTH	NA	$2,730,744	$3,968,7
OPEX GROWTH	NA	$1,908,072	$499,53

	YEAR 1	YEAR 2	YEAR
YoY MARGIN GROWTH	NA	$822,671	$3,469,2
YoY MARGIN GROWTH	NA	-34.41%	31.71%

ENTERPRISE VALUE	YEAR 1	YEAR 2	YEAR
6X REVENUE	$3,676,195	$20,060,657	$43,873,5
8X REVENUE	$4,901,599	$26,747,543	$58,497,7
10X REVENUE	$6,126,991	$33,434,429	$73,122,1
12X REVENUE	$7,352,389	$40,121,314	$87,746,6
15X REVENUE	$9,190,487	$50,151,643	$109,683,

NOTES

LISTING EVENT ON ASX POSSIBLE IN YEAR 4, WHICH COULD BE SELF-FINANCING

ALTERNATIVE LISTING EVENT ON THE LSE IN LONDON IN YEAR 4, WHICH AGAIN COULD BE SELF FINANCED

BUSINESS WOULD BECOME AN ACQUISITION TARGET IN YEAR 3. BY MEDIA, MARKET RESEARCH, JOB SEARCH AND TECH PLATFORM PLAYERS

LICENSING/PARTNERSHIPS REVENUE RECOGNISED MONTHLY

R&D GRANT CALCULATED AT APPROXIMATELY 40% OF TECH AND MANAGEMENT COST

ANNUAL REVENUE METRICS

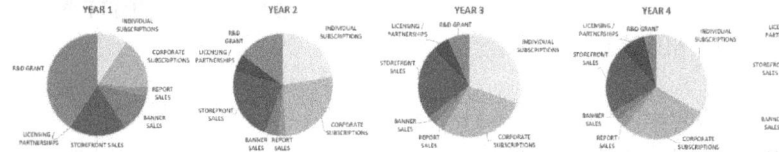

MONTHLY TRAVEL

The 'Monthly Travel' page outlines how the business performs on a monthly basis, taking into account the various costs and revenue models included.

Think of it as a monthly breakdown of the 'Results Page', enabling you to see how the business trends during the year. This is especially important for subscription-businesses, where annual subscription sales have to be broken down and recognised on a monthly basis.

Additionally, this page enables you to see if anything odd crops up during the building process. It is great as a sanity checker.

The attributes for this page are slightly different and roll out across the page from month one through to month 60 for a 5-year model.

The attributes include:

- → PERSONAL SUBSCRIPTIONS
- → COMPANY SUBSCRIPTIONS
- → SINGLE COPY REPORT SALES
- → BANNER SALES
- → STOREFRONT SALES
- → LICENSING / PARTNERSHIPS
- → R&D GRANT
- → MONTHLY TOTALS
- → MARKETING SPEND
- → HR COSTS
- → OFFICE AND ADMINISTRATION COSTS
- → FINANCE AND PROFESSIONAL SERVICES COSTS
- → TOTAL OPEX
- → EBIT ($)
- → EBIT (%)
- → MONTHLY GROWTH RATE – REVENUE
- → MONTHLY GROWTH RATE – OPEX
- → MONTHLY GROWTH RATE – MARGIN
- → YoY GROWTH RATE – REVENUE
- → YoY GROWTH RATE – OPEX
- → VISITS
- → PAGE VIEWS
- → PAGE VIEWS PER VISIT
- → BANNER IMPRESSIONS
- → MONTHLY GROWTH - VISITORS
- → YoY GROWTH – VISITORS
- → MONTHLY GROWTH – PAGE VIEWS
- → YoY GROWTH - PAGE VIEWS
- → MONTHLY GROWTH – PAGE VIEWS PER VISIT
- → YoY GROWTH – PAGE VIEWS PER VISIT

INDIVIDUAL SUBSCRIPTIONS MODEL

The 'Individual Subscriptions Model' page is broken down by month and utilises the following model variables:

→ AVERAGE MONTHLY SUBSCRIPTION COST
→ AVERAGE DISCOUNT ON PRICE
→ RESULTING MONTHLY SUBSCRIPTION COST
→ AVERAGE MONTHLY RETENTION RATE
→ FREE TO PAID CONVERSION RATE
→ FREE TRIAL PERIOD (in months)
→ VIRTUAL REALITY – TRIALS PER MONTH
→ SPACE TECHNOLOGY – TRIALS PER MONTH
→ GENOMICS – TRIALS PER MONTH
→ AI – TRIALS PER MONTH
→ ALTERNATIVE ENERGY – TRIALS PER MONTH
→ NANOTECHNOLOGY – TRIALS PER MONTH
→ PHARMACEUTICAL TECHNOLOGY – TRIALS PER MONTH
→ VIRTUAL REALITY – PAID SIGN-UPS
→ SPACE TECHNOLOGY – PAID SIGN-UPS
→ GENOMICS - PAID SIGN-UPS
→ AI – PAID SIGN-UPS
→ ALTERNATIVE ENERGY – PAID SIGN-UPS
→ NANOTECHNOLOGY – PAID SIGN-UPS
→ PHARMACEUTICAL TECHNOLOGY – PAID SIGN-UPS

As the example business we are talking about is a new product, you will need to include build time and any resulting lag into the model. Assume the same for the 'Corporate Subscriptions Model' and the 'Advertising Sales' pages. The resource available and complexity of the build to MVP status would dictate to you the build time and resulting lag. This could be anything from 3-6 months.

The model is separated into the following sections:

FREE TRIAL VARIABLES

→ VIRTUAL REALITY – TRIALS PER MONTH
→ SPACE TECHNOLGOY – TRIALS PER MONTH
→ GENOMICS – TRIALS PER MONTH
→ AI – TRIALS PER MONTH
→ ALTERNATIVE ENERGY – TRIALS PER MONTH
→ NANOTECHNOLOGY – TRIALS PER MONTH
→ PHARMACEUTICAL TECHNOLOGY – TRIALS PER MONTH
→ TOTAL TRIALS PER MONTH

PAID MODEL – SIGN-UP VARIABLES

→ VIRTUAL REALITY – PAID SIGN-UPS
→ SPACE TECHNOLOGY – PAID SIGN-UPS
→ GENOMICS – PAID SIGN-UPS
→ AI – PAID SIGN-UPS
→ ALTERNATIVE ENERGY – PAID SIGN-UPS
→ NANOTECHNOLOGY – PAID SIGN-UPS
→ PHARMACEUTICAL TECHNOLOGY – PAID SIGN-UPS
→ TOTAL SIGN-UPS PER MONTH

FREE TRIALS – MONTHLY MATURING

→ VIRTUAL REALITY
→ SPACE TECHNOLOGY
→ GENOMICS
→ AI
→ ALTERNATIVE ENERGY
→ NANOTECHNOLOGY
→ PHARMACEUTICAL TECHNOLOGY
→ TOTAL

PAID USERS – MONTHLY TOTALS

➔ VIRTUAL REALITY
➔ SPACE TECHNOLOGY
➔ GENOMICS
➔ AI
➔ ALTERNATIVE ENERGY
➔ NANOTECHNOLOGY
➔ PHARMACEUTICAL TECHNOLOGY
➔ TOTAL

TOTAL MONTHLY REVENUES

➔ VIRTUAL REALITY
➔ SPACE TECHNOLOGY
➔ GENOMICS
➔ AI
➔ ALTERNATIVE ENERGY
➔ NANOTECHNOLOGY
➔ PHARMACEUTICAL TECHNOLOGY
➔ TOTAL REVENUE

RESULTING ANNUAL REVENUES

➔ VIRTUAL REALITY – BY YEAR
➔ SPACE TECHNOLOGY – BY YEAR
➔ GENOMICS – BY YEAR
➔ AI – BY YEAR
➔ ALTERNATIVE ENERGY – BY YEAR
➔ NANOTECHNOLOGY – BY YEAR
➔ PHARMACEUTICAL TECHNOLOGY – BY YEAR
➔ TOTAL REVENUE – BY YEAR

Finally, it is worth remembering that users Credit Card information is garnered during the free trial sign-up process. –More on this later in the book.

CORPORATE SUBSCRIPTIONS MODEL

The 'Corporate Subscription' we use for the example business is a slightly easier product to model, as it does not include free trials and resulting conversion rates. As a result the following are variables that we will use to construct the rolling monthly model:

➜ AVERAGE MONTHLY SUBSCRIPTION COST
➜ AVERAGE DISCOUNT ON PRICE
➜ RESULTING MONTHLY SUBSCRIPTION COST
➜ AVERAGE MONTHLY RETENTION RATE

In addition to the standard variables, the model makes use of paid sign-up variables to power the other numbers. These can be predicted from the marketing results, et alia.

Personally, I am always conservative with these numbers as they cannot be known for new products.

PAID MODEL – MONTHLY SIGN-UP VARIABLES

➜ VIRTUAL REALITY
➜ SPACE TECHNOLOGY
➜ GENOMICS
➜ AI
➜ ALTERNATIVE ENERGY
➜ NANOTECHNOLOGY
➜ PHARMACEUTICAL TECHNOLOGY
➜ TOTAL SIGN-UPS PER MONTH

PAID USERS - MONTHLY TOTALS

➜ VIRTUAL REALITY
➜ SPACE TECHNOLOGY
➜ GENOMICS
➜ AI
➜ ALTERNATIVE ENERGY
➜ NANOTECHNOLOGY
➜ PHARMACEUTICAL TECHNOLOGY
➜ TOTAL REVENUE

RESULTING MONTHLY REVENUES

➜ VIRTUAL REALITY
➜ SPACE TECHNOLOGY
➜ GENOMICS
➜ AI
➜ ALTERNATIVE ENERGY
➜ NANOTECHNOLOGY
➜ PHARMACEUTICAL TECHNOLOGY
➜ TOTAL MONTHLY REVENUE

RESULTING ANNUAL REVENUES

➜ VIRTUAL REALITY
➜ SPACE TECHNOLOGY
➜ GENOMICS
➜ AI
➜ ALTERNATIVE ENERGY
➜ NANOTECHNOLOGY
➜ PHARMACEUTICAL TECHNOLOGY
➜ TOTAL ANNUAL REVENUE

As with the 'Individual Subscriptions' page the 'Corporate Subscriptions' model plugs the annual numbers into the 'Results Page' and the monthly numbers into the 'Budget Detail' and 'Monthly Travel' worksheets.

REPORT SALES

The 'Report Sales' worksheet outlines the various report products that the example business will take to market. It takes into account both internally produced reports; and those produced externally by a separate vendor such as Gartner, or GlobalData and then sold by the business.

The model variables that we use with the 'Report Sales' model are as follows:

- ➜ PRICE OF COMPANY PROFILES (SWOTS ON DEMAND)
- ➜ PRICE OF QUARTERLY REPORTS
- ➜ PRICE OF INDUSTRY PROFILES
- ➜ PRICE OF MANAGEMENT REPORTS
- ➜ AVERAGE VALUE OF EXTERNAL REPORT
- ➜ PERCENTAGE REVENUE PER SALE

In addition to the standard variables, we also feature a rolling monthly variable based around a cautious, yet steadily ramped-up sales effort, noting the small initial size of the marketing lists, amongst other reasons.

The variables are for the entire period of the model, so in this case 60 months and unlike the other commercial models are not broken down by individual portal.

The reasoning for this is that by utilising the slice and dice methodology outlined elsewhere in this book the business will likely produce R&A reports not strictly fitting within the defined niche markets covered by the portals.

→ REPORT SALES PER MONTH
→ COMPANY PROFILES (SWOTS ON DEMAND)
→ QUARTERLY REPORTS
→ INDUSTRY PROFILES
→ MANAGEMENT REPORTS
→ 3RD PARTY PREMIUM REPORTS

The variables highlighted above generate the following results:

RESULTING MONTHLY REVENUE

→ COMPANY PROFILES (SWOTS ON DEMAND)
→ QUARTERLY REPORTS
→ INDUSTRY PROFILES
→ MANAGEMENT REPORTS
→ 3RD PARTY PREMIUM REPORTS
→ TOTAL MONTHLY REVENUE

RESULTING ANNUAL REVENUE

→ COMPANY PROFILES (SWOTS ON DEMAND)
→ QUARTERLY REPORTS
→ INDUSTRY PROFILES
→ MANAGEMENT REPORTS
→ 3RD PARTY PREMIUM REPORTS
→ TOTAL ANNUAL REVENUE

ADVERTISING SALES

The advertising model consists of both standard marketing services efforts, such as internal and third-party inventory sales; and also company listings, which for our example business we are calling Storefronts.

In terms of banner inventory variables, I do not break it down by ad unit, only by the average value of the inventory. This methodology behind this calculation can be as simple, or as exacting as you wish. In-short, I tend to go with a calculation based on CPM value of the units displayed on the page, divided by the number of units. The average is simply the resulting number.

The variables for this section of the page as therefore as follows:

→ AVERAGE VALUE OF AD (IN-HOUSE)
→ AVERAGE VALUE OF AD (3RD PARTY)
→ IN-HOUSE INVENTORY SOLD
→ 3RD PARTY INVENTORY SOLD

Now we move on to the variables we will use for our directory listing 'Storefront' product. As the product itself is license driven and sold (with an auto-renew) over a 12 month period, I simplify the model by stating the monthly cost of the license. Also for simplicity I use a monthly retention rate.

Both of these simplifications actually add flexibility to the model and sales methodology.

The variables used for this section are:

→ MONTHLY COST
→ MONTHLY RETENTION RATE
→ SALES PER PERSON (PER MONTH)

I then break the Storefront sales effort down by month... and include the following key variables which will enable the business to return results in the sheet:

→ STOREFRONT SALES HEADCOUNT
→ ROLLING STOREFRONTS

I then move back to the inventory sales effort and note traffic, which are inputted from the 'Marketing Plan' page of the workbook. The results shown here are:

→ UNIQUE BROWSERS
→ VISITS
→ PAGE VIEWS
→ PAGE VIEWS PER VISIT
→ BANNER IMPRESSIONS

From this traffic we then calculate the monthly revenue totals for the entire 'Advertising Sales' effort, broken down as follows:

RESULTING MONTHLY REVENUE

→ IN-HOUSE INVENTORY SALES
→ THIRD-PARTY INVENTORY SALES
→ STOREFRONT SALES (RECOGNISED)
→ MONTHLY TOTAL

ANNUAL REVENUE

→ IN-HOUSE INVENTORY SALES
→ THIRD-PARTY INVENTORY SALES
→ STOREFRONT SALES
→ TOTAL REVENUE

Reminder: with the 'Advertising Sales' numbers a lag and platform development time needs to be built into the equation.

MARKETING PLAN

For obvious reasons the 'Marketing Plan' is important to the accuracy of the entire business. Without an audience our example business will not work. In-fact, without a suitable audience, no online business will work.

The worksheet consists of a monthly matrix for the entire duration of the model. In the example case its 60 months. These months are then separated into blocks of 12, as per years. It will be easier to do this last of all so as speed up the development of the model.

The plan then features what we will call 'Group Spend Variables', covering each and every marketing spend, per month, minus headcount. The variables include the following:

→ GOOGLE ADWORDS
→ BING
→ YAHOO
→ OTHER PPC
→ TWITTER
→ GOOGLE DISPLAY NETWORK / REMARKETING
→ FACEBOOK ADS
→ STUMBLEUPON
→ LINKEDIN
→ NEW INITIATIVES
→ OTHER TRAFFIC SOURCES
→ LEAD GENERATION

Once we have set the (initial) breakdown monthly budget spend for the above we then look at the audience variables. These consist of the following:

→ ORGANIC MONTHLY GROWTH RATE *
→ GENERIC SOURCE – PAGE VIEWS PER VISIT
→ GOOGLE ADWORDS – PAGE VIEWS PER VISIT

➜ FACEBOOK – PAGE VIEWS PER VISIT
➜ GOOGLE DISPLAY – PAGE VIEWS PER VISIT
➜ STARTING VISITS – GROUP
➜ CONTENT MARKETING – VISITS PER ARTICLE
➜ CONTENT MARKETING – COST PER ARTICLE

* With the 'Organic Monthly Growth Rate' number it will be worth including seasonality in the numbers.

Additional variables relating to audience are also needed so the model should include the following. Add/edit/delete where needed depending upon the desired spend:

➜ AVERAGE CPC – ADWORDS
➜ AVERAGE CPC – FACEBOOK
➜ AVERAGE CPC – BING
➜ AVERAGE CPC – YAHOO
➜ AVERAGE CPC - GOOGLE DISPLAY
➜ AVERAGE CPC – OTHER
➜ CPC – STUMBLEUPON
➜ AVERAGE BANNERS PER PAGE

By implementing these variables we can garner the 'Group Spend Results' data, broken down by month.

➜ PRESS RELEASES
➜ EMAIL BROADCASTING
➜ GOOGLE ADWORDS
➜ YAHOO SPEND
➜ BING SPEND
➜ TWITTER SPEND
➜ OTHER PPC
➜ CONTENT MARKETING
➜ STUMBLEUPON
➜ LINKEDIN

→ OTHER TRAFFIC CAMPAIGNS
→ LEAD GENERATION
→ FACEBOOK ADS
→ GOOGLE DISPLAY NETWORK
→ HOOTSUITE
→ CRM LICENSE
→ NEW INITIATIVES
→ TOTAL SPEND

Additionally, we also get a prognostication of the monthly traffic numbers:

→ UNIQUE BROWSERS
→ VISITS
→ PAGE VIEWS
→ PAGE VIEWS PER USER
→ BANNER IMPRESSIONS

CONTRIBUTOR PAYMENT MODEL

The 'Contributor Payment Model' sheet is designed to calculate the editorial spend required to support the business.

Broken down by month, the model variables included in the model are as follows:

→ NUMBER OF ARTICLES PER MONTH
→ ARTICLES PER MONTH - VIRTUAL REALITY
→ ARTICLES PER MONTH - SPACE TECHNOLOGY
→ ARTICLES PER MONTH - GENOMICS
→ ARTICLES PER MONTH - AI
→ ARTICLES PER MONTH - ALTERNATIVE ENERGY
→ ARTICLES PER MONTH - NANOTECHNOLOGY

➜ ARTICLES PER MONTH - PHARMACEUTICAL
TECHNOLOGY

BASE PAYMENT RATES

➜ BONUS RATE 1
➜ BONUS RATE 2
➜ BONUS RATE 3
➜ BONUS RATE 4
➜ BONUS RATE 5
➜ BONUS RATE 6
➜ BONUS RATE 7
➜ BONUS RATE 8
➜ BONUS RATE 9
➜ BONUS RATE 10
➜ BONUS RATE 11

The variables drive the following monthly and annual cost results:

➜ VIRTUAL REALITY
➜ SPACE TECHNOLOGY
➜ GENOMICS
➜ AI
➜ ALTERNATIVE ENERGY
➜ NANOTECHNOLOGY
➜ PHARMACEUTICAL TECHNOLOGY
➜ TOTAL CONTRIBUTOR COST

HR COSTS

This worksheet includes a list of all employees who will likely be employed during the duration of the 60 month model. Emphasis is placed on the first 18-months in order to get the model as accurately as possible.

To enable better categorisation and analysis of resources each employee is broken down by business unit, locale, type of resource, type of employee (FTE, PT, Contractor, et alia), salary, allowances, bonuses and pay rise percentage for future years (including inflation).

The table calculates both the monthly and annual cost per employee.

The variables include:

➔ 12 MONTH PAY INCREASE
➔ PAYRISES ARE GIVEN ANNUALLY, AFTER EACH 12 MONTHS OF EMPLOYMENT

ADDITIONAL PAYROLL COSTS

➔ SUPERANNUATION
➔ PAYROLL TAX
➔ WORKCOVER
➔ TOTAL COSTS

Other costs included in this sheet are Directors fees, and commission.

To calculate the total commission number we use variables for the following attributes:

➔ SALES PERSON
➔ SALES MANAGER
➔ SALES DIRECTOR

ASSORTED COSTS

The 'Assorted Costs' sheet includes monthly and annual breakdowns of costs not included elsewhere in the model. These costs are best organised into two categories:

→ OFFICE AND ADMINISTRATION
→ FINANCE AND PROFESSIONAL SERVICES

Again, the costs include inflation for future years.

BUDGET DETAIL

The 'Budget Detail' page operates in the same way as a standard Profit and Loss document. It highlights and predicts all monthly costs and revenues, broken down first by month and then by year.

CONTENT MATRIX

The 'Content Matrix as discussed in more detail elsewhere within this book. It is included in the workbook to highlight more detail with the business and visually explain what the content spend returns.

CHAPTER 5

Product Development

P roduct development as a task may involve simply modifying an pre-existing product, or its look and feel. Alternatively, it can mean the creation of an entirely new product that satisfies a market niche, or potential opportunity.

In terms of our example portals business, the aim of our product development activity is to create new products and services in order to establish and then dominate the emerging technology industry verticals.

New Product Development

New product development (NPD) can be best explained and broken down in the following way:

CONCEPT – This is the new idea. The disruptive concept. The innovation upon an existing product. Basically put, it's where the product begins.

RESEARCH – Is a similar product available elsewhere? What is the competitive landscape like? Are IP protections in place to stop the development?

Researching not just the competitive landscape but also the industry as a whole for developments is key to understanding the viability of the product before the (more costly) development stage.

PRODUCT DEVELOPMENT – Product development within online portals normally starts with prototyping and wireframes.

Once the prototyping of the product has been completed and the final specification agreed then the product development activity moves into production-mode. For most portal-based businesses this can be anywhere from three months through to one year for MVP.

During this stage, I have always found it wise to start content production. It will enable the business to launch with a more attractive initial proposition and make the most of any initial view, or review of the business by both peers and industry insiders.

TESTING – Once the development nears the end of its cycle the business will want to test various iterations of the product. This will improve usability, resource usage, performance, error checking and sales funnel performance.

Beta testing is one option available to the business as it could offer access for a strictly limited number of people to review and benchmark performance and any issues encountered during this phase. Focus groups both external and internal are also an option here.

Remember, testing is all about learning.

PRODUCT LAUNCH – This is the final stage of new product development... and perhaps the most glamorous part.

The business launches the portal to the general public and starts marketing and implementing commercial strategies.

Creating any new product is difficult and a risk. This is especially the case with subscription-based products making use of a relatively expensive production cost. Product development however is not merely about navigating the stages of new product development. It is also very much about successfully managing a product through its lifecycle.

Product Lifecycle

There are four stages in the lifetime of a product:

LAUNCH – The introduction of any new product into the marketplace is the first stage of its lifecycle.

GROWTH – This is the stage where once launched and established within the marketplace the subscriptions garnered and churn rate is minimal. It is during this period that further investment into the next iteration of the product takes place.

MATURITY – At this stage of the product lifecycle, the product hits its potential. In the case of our example membership portals then this either equates to maxing out on the number of subscribers, or the period where the product is at its most competitive in the industry and of most use to subscribers.

DECLINE – This is the final stage in the lifecycle of a product. A products decline could be down to market saturation within the field, a change of emphasis in the industry, or simply a more competitive (better) product being available to potential purchasers.

If you do not have the next iteration of the product ready by this stage, its potentially game over.

The Kona Model and Process

Kano is a product development theory that classifies features into five simple areas to aid prioritisation. By classifying functionality and design aspects into these five categories designers can deliver tangible innovation effectively.

1. **MUST HAVE** – These are what you would describe as the minimum expected functionality... or minimum viable product. Users take these functions for granted, but disappointed if they are absent.

2. **ONE DIMENSIONAL** – These are features that are received differently by user depending upon how well (or badly) they are implemented. Users will likely be excited if they are implemented well and disappointed if they are not.

3. **ATTRACTIVE** – These are features that are unexpected. Users of the property will be excited if they are present, but not disappointed if they are absent from the build.

4. **INDIFFERENT** – These are features that will neither excite nor disappoint the portals user. In other words, they are boring.

5. **REVERSE** – These are rather divisive. The reception to them depends upon the individual portal user. When present some users will love them, others will be somewhat disappointed.

Developing a Roadmap

A product roadmap offers a broad overview of all aspects of an upcoming product: mission goals, timeline, features, resource needed, et alia.

The roadmap indicates (1) what the web development team is building; (2) the problem the new functionality, or content type will solve; and (3) the business goals for the product.

Additionally, it should be noted that effective product roadmaps also serve as a fundamental strategic and communications asset when managing products. It offers the business owner a unique perspective on where the product is; where the product will be; and how to get there.

As part of the product development activity, the product roadmap should be developed early on, communicated at all levels within the business and understood in full, at all times. This way the business knows what direction they are travelling in.

Every manager will have his, or her preferred product roadmap flavour. Personally, I prefer to view it in three separate formats.

1. **MS WORD FORMAT** – Including top-level descriptions of the initiatives

2. **GANTT CHART** – This enables me to visualise the timeframes, reliance and prognosticate potential risks ahead. Gantt charts in general are a great way of understanding the project operations of a business.

3. **POWERPOINT** – This enables me to format for Board meetings, or for potential investors as it can visually explains the actual and planned activities effectively

CHAPTER 6

Platform Development

This section of the book outlines various strategies and functionality that will increase the potential, the quality and the usage of the platform.

The *most* vital functionality described here is the Metered Paywall, which is discussed in detail throughout the book.

In addition to this, I have added some of what I consider the more forward-looking functionality and website features. These fully embrace the direction the content business is going... and will give this business a unique platform and proposition.

Technology Set-up

A proprietary content management system will be built in order to manage the AI and data sets effectively. This CMS will be e-commerce enabled, offer cross-platform support for phone, tablets as well as desktops.

Each individual portal will share the same admin area in order to enable content items, when/where necessary to be published on more than the one site at a time.

Additionally, portions of the portal will be powered by the Apache SOLR enterprise search engine. This will enable a faceted search and to increase the relationship between registered users, individual content items, the taxonomy, et cetera.

The entirety of the platform will be hosted within a secure (SSL) environment and require username (Email address) and password to access the content. All files and content items will be hosted in the cloud.

Protecting the IP

The business should attempt to garner trademarks in relevant countries for all of the brands it will operate.

Additionally, any platform-based business with unique, proprietary technology, such as the business outlined in this book should attempt to protect its unique IP. To achieve this it will be worth investigating the potential to receive an International (PCT) Patent.

The aim of doing this is not simply down to the protections, or licensing opportunities that a Patent can offer. Instead, as the application process takes years, the application itself can add value of the enterprise.

PCT Patents cost about AU$18,000 and can be applied for directly, or via an agency that will manage the process and documentation requirements on your behalf.

Metered Paywall

The Metered Paywall is amongst the most popular methodologies for subscription-based businesses, having been originally been pioneered within the digital publishing space by the FT back in the late 1990's.

Today, the majority of the larger-scale financially successful newspapers and magazine properties utilise the model as it (1) enables the publisher to vastly increase its potential audience by opening up the site to Search Engines such as Google, to social media properties like Twitter, Facebook, et cetera; and (2) it enables self-selecting conversions, where if a user is already accessing the property then that user likely values it and is thus more likely to want to continue to use it.

In-short, the Metered Paywall allows digital publishers to offer visitors a certain number of free articles per month, complete with unobtrusive reminder after which a 'velvet rope' is lowered. To access any more content during the defined time span then the visitor must pay.

No implementation of a Metered Paywall will be alike. The number of free to access articles each property will be offer... and of what content type... and over what timeframe will be different. These are vital decisions that any publisher within the membership economy will have to decide.

Continued research and analysis will need to be carried out with existing users to ensure that you do not lose members because of the limited free access.

Core Functionality

Below is a concise list of the functionality required as part of a Metered Paywall solution for the membership platform. The functions that have been listed act as MVP for subscriptions management:

METERED ACCESS – The basis of the paywall is the ability to limit the number of articles based on cookies.

MULTI-LEVEL SUBSCRIPTIONS – This gives the property flexibility in its subscription offering.

For example, you can have 3-month, 12 month subscriptions, or PAYG monthly subscriptions to a nanotechnology site, to a genomics-based site, or for all.

API TO EMAIL – The paywall will need to integrate with whatever Email broadcasting system you choose to use, such as Mail Chimp.

ARTICLE NAGS – A fundamental part of the Metered Paywall model is the ability for present an article countdown.

For example, if you were to offer the visitor 3x page views per month free access then each of those three pages should have a countdown nag on them telling the user that they only have 3, 2, 1 articles left.

MULTI-DOMAIN – The paywall will need to work both on all the various websites within the network. Additionally, it will need to be able to work on sub-domains.

IP EXCEPTIONS – This will enable people in the office to continue to have full access. Additionally, it will allow you to sell subscriptions to libraries, et cetera. –Commercially, this could be a good new revenue stream.

SUBSCRIPTION MANAGEMENT – The ability to add, edit and search subscribers.

BUSINESS RULES – The solution will need to be able to handle different types of content, with different privileges.

For example, the website may offer a free report, but only to paid subscribers.

CLEAN SEF URL'S – The URL of each content item must remain as is; and free from redirects. I have dealt with URL's that included redirects based on user session within them. –Absolute disaster.

CMS INTEGRATION – The paywall solution will need to integrate seamlessly with the CMS. This means that the editor can set the rules quickly and easily (or the dev team can set them automagically) depending upon strategy.

REPORTING – Management will need to know exactly how many subscribers each vortal has at any one time… and importantly for marketing, what the usage of that subscriber is… when the subscription term is up… et alia.

GATEWAY – The paywall must integrate with the existing payment gateway.

Additional Paywall Functionality

Along with the core functionality of a Metered Paywall, the functions below are deemed important for the platform:

COUPON GENERATION – The ability to create coupons opens up a number of options for the platform. In-short, with this functionality you create the possibility to offer a new Student subscription... along with discount offers for specific users.

GIFT SUBSCRIPTIONS – In my opinion this functionality is vital. The functionality behind this enables a third party to purchase a subscription on behalf of somebody else, thus increasing the potential of the site. In-turn, this enables businesses, government, or NGO's to buy a subscription based on a 'seats' model.

Exploring Voice and Visual Interfaces

I have a firm belief that the historical internet-era design interface paradigm is beginning to change. It is moving away from purely the visual, be it mobile-friendly responsive, or via static navigation and towards something more intelligent, immersive and instant.

In the coming few years publishing platforms will feature both traditional menu-based navigation and a flexible voice-activated interactive navigation cross-platform.

The key principles of the interface design are as described in the sections below:

Structure

The design should organize the user interface purposefully, in meaningful and useful ways based on clear, consistent models that are apparent and recognizable to users, putting related things together and separating unrelated things, differentiating dissimilar things and making similar things resemble one another. The structure principle is concerned with overall user interface architecture

Simplicity

The interfaces design should make simple, common tasks easy, communicating clearly and simply in the user's own language, and providing good shortcuts that are meaningfully related to longer procedures

Visibility

The design should make all needed options and materials for a given task visible without distracting the user with extraneous or redundant information. Good designs don't overwhelm users with alternatives or confuse with unneeded information.

Feedback

The design of the platforms interface should keep users informed of actions or interpretations, changes of state or condition, and errors or exceptions that are relevant and of interest to the user through clear, concise, and unambiguous language familiar to users.

Tolerance

The interface design should be flexible and tolerant, reducing the cost of mistakes and misuse by allowing undoing and redoing, while also preventing errors wherever possible by tolerating varied inputs and sequences and by interpreting all reasonable actions.

Reuse

The design of the interface should reuse internal and external components and behaviours, maintaining consistency with purpose rather than merely arbitrary consistency, thus reducing the need for users to rethink and remember.

Coding: Keep it Clean and Elegant

The below is a quick outline of best practices and what to look out for when reviewing code:

➜ Plan everything prior to execution
➜ Implement functions and classes
➜ Commenting and documentation, even if the team deem it obvious
➜ Use loops and arrays
➜ Consistent indentation style and naming schemes
➜ Avoid creating too many levels to the code
➜ Create separate blocks of code within the file

➜ DIY – don't repeat yourself
➜ Make it easy for a human to read and decipher
➜ Maintain a file and folder structure
➜ Separate the code from data
➜ Refactor code
➜ Test and debug as you go
➜ Implement version control

Server Speed and Locale

One of the crucial factors with any platform is the time it takes to load in the users' browser/client. Assuming the server specification is acceptable and the web server is separated away from the database server; or that you have allocated enough resource within the cloud, much of the speed equation is down to the software specification. Here is where decisions must be made.

For example, if you feature too many database pulls; inefficient, or too much code; or perhaps errors with server-side or browser caching, the time the website takes to load and the resource usage required to load it will slow the site down to a crawl. In extreme cases it can even crash the site.

Within the content business, speed is key. I am impatient to read content. You too are likely to be impatient to read an article, especially if you find it from a Search Engine, or via social media. If it takes more than a few seconds, people move on.

This is the same case for e-commerce properties too. Famously, the shopping platform Shopzilla generated 12 per cent more revenue by simply reducing the time it takes for the website to render from six seconds down to about one second.

In terms of server location, it is wise to have either co-location, or (preferably) be part of a cloud network.

The use of global content delivery networks (CDN) like MaxCDN, or Amazon is likely required too, especially if the platform is image, or file heavy. These cloud-based networks speed up delivery of files by serving the content item from the location nearest to the visitor.

SSL Certificates

Moving-forward Google is likely to require all websites to move to a secure server. This will mean some disruption for content, or e-commerce-based businesses as they will need to migrate all pages from http://... To https://...

Google is likely to start actively penalising businesses that are not utilising a secure server for all pages sometime in 2018. Other traffic sources are likely to follow quickly behind.

It is therefore recommended that any existing platforms migrate as soon as convenient... and all new platforms utilise a secure domain.

Acquire the best SSL certificate you can for all the portal domains and subdomains. This means, 2048 bit encryption, complete with 'extended validation', which reassures visitors by turning the address bar green in browsers.

E-commerce

The platform is transactional, with each portal able to accept credit card payments for both subscription-based products and also for single-copy R&A report products.

As a subscription business it is a requirement that the portal and the Merchant account the business is using is set-up to take and process recurring charges.

Core Functionality

Below is a list outlining the core functionality involved in an effective e-commerce engine:

SECURITY – The entirety of the portal will be behind a secure server.

MULTIPLE DESIGN OPTIONS – The design of the product item and product list pages must be adaptable. The business will undertake constant A/B and multivariate testing to ensure that conversions are optimised.

PRODUCT MANAGEMENT – The metadata for the products should be easily manageable.

SEO – The product item pages should be optimised for Search Engines. Combined with high quality metadata this will create opportunity for high quality free, organic search traffic.

To ensure that the site offers the best potential performance the pages should offer a static URL wherever possible.

SHOPPING CART – If the platform was offering purely subscriptions, or a single product no shopping cart would be needed. However, as the portals will market not only subscriptions, but also potentially thousands of products within each vertical a shopping cart will be needed.

For example, a user may want to purchase a SWOT analysis for 5-10 of its competitors or acquisition targets within the space.

CLEAN CODE – As with all other aspects of the platform, the code base needs to be clean and efficient.

SEARCH INTEGRATION – Any platform-based business integrating an e-commerce store that offers a number of different products will need to utilise a facetted enterprise-level Search Engine such as Apache SOLR, or the like.

In addition to offering relevant search results based on product type and scope, the enterprise-class search will also enable the business to better relate products together. Returning the most relevant 'Related Reports' back to the visitor as possible.

FAQ'S – This enables the business to answer any pre-purchase questions; remove potential objections; and to help the user understand the products.

CHATBOTS – Integrating Chatbots, such as Live Chat functionality with the e-commerce pages enables the business to convert more visitors into purchasers. Additionally, it helps address objections to purchasing and opens a dialogue.

Product Presentation

When selling single-copy R&A reports, the key thing to remember is to feature all the information that is required to convince the visitor to make a purchase on the product page.

This can be achieved by linking to the Table of Contents, the Table of Figures and Marketing Brochure all from that one item page. When the clicks on one of these links a new window opens. It goes without saying that this is vital, as you do not want the lead to move away from the purchase page.

The full list of metadata that is required for the product page is as follows:

REPORT TITLE – It is vital that the report title is keyword rich, specific and has a relationship to the SEF URL.

PRICE – It goes without saying that you want the end user to be able to see the pricing structure of the report product. Please note that I use the words 'pricing structure', as most single-copy R&A products have different prices depending upon use.

For example, if only one person is to use the report then the price will be X. If the report will be accessed by an office, or department then the price will be Y. If however, the report is to be accessed across the entire organisation then the price will be Z.

PUBLISHED DATE – The date that the research was published, or updated. You need only bother with the month and year, as the specific day is rarely required. Always go with the latest genuine date possible as you are trying to build relevance. Many R&A vendors review and update reports every few months in order to maximise the relevance to potential purchasers.

FORMAT – This is where you tell the visitor whether the R&A item is an Excel model, a PDF, or something else.

TABLE OF CONTENTS – As mentioned previously, including a ToC, marketing materials and list of figures can aid in persuading the potential purchaser to buy the report. It is vital that as many of these as available are included on the product page.

It is worthwhile making these pages printable so that the potential purchaser can view them offline. This is especially vital on R&A products that have a high ticket price... because a high ticket price often requires additional sign-off from the management of the business.

INTRODUCTION – This is a short, sharp few sentences that best introduce the report to potential purchasers. The metadata for this section can be formula-driven and compiled using Excel, much in the same way that you would write a templated Email campaign.

For example you could construct a template and then simply insert the title, insert the publisher, the target sector, date, et cetera.

SCOPE OF THE REPORT – The section of the marketing that outlines what the report covers. It also highlights who it is aimed at. As a result the scope should always be prepared by the author.

REPORT HIGHLIGHTS – This section can be longer and include some of the key findings you would include in the marketing brochure and/or the Executive Summary. However, it is important to be selective here and not go into any real depth.

REASONS TO PURCHASE – When preparing marketing for products I always have this in mind. Take your time and prioritise the reasons into a list of 6-7 line items. Keep each line item to one sentence and make those sentences as powerful as possible.

From experience in selling R&A reports, this is the key attribute of the page. You are telling the potential purchaser what problem this report solves.

Additionally, I would always recommend having the following attributes available on the page:

BREADCRUMB TRAIL – Use the taxonomy of the site to enable your users to quickly and easily navigate to other report-based products that may be of relevance to them. This is especially important in vertical industry portals.

LEAD GENERATION FORM – This is a short prefilled form that enables the business to capture the details of any visitor that is interested in purchasing the report. The details of the form should be pre-filled with the report title, date/time, referrer and (if a member) the users details.

If the lead is not a member then the user will need to be able to complete the form, which consists of the following fields:

- → Full name
- → Job title
- → Company
- → Telephone
- → Email
- → Enquiry

RELATED PRODUCTS – This is a section of the page, appearing either below the product, or to the right-hand side of the product that displays a limited number of products that may be of interest to the potential purchaser.

The Related Reports functionality could be powered by an Enterprise-class search engine such as Apache SOLR, or similar. Simply use the facetted search to return the relevant results here.

CHATBOT INTEGRATION – It is imperative that the page features a Chatbot, such as Live Chat functionality that pops up after the visitor has lingered for more than 20 seconds on the page. This will generate live leads for the sales team, even if the visitor is in an entirely separate time-zone.

The key to success with Chatbots is to ensure that the script you provide to the supplier is bulletproof and aims to garner the contact details (minimum of name, company Email and/or call back number) and the name of the specific report they are interested in purchasing.

BREADCRUMB TRAIL >> BREADCRUMB TRAIL >> BREADCRUMB TRAIL >> BREADCRUMB TRAIL

REPORT TITLE

Quantity in Basket: None

ADD TO BASKET   **BUY NOW**

PRICE: $$$$$$

REPORT FORMAT: XXXXXXX
DATE PUBLISHED: XXXXXXXXXX
PRODUCT TYPE: XXXXXXXXXXX
TABLE OF CONTENTS: CLICK HERE

INTRODUCTION:

Lorem ipsum dolor sit amet, consectetur adipiscing elit, sed do eiusmod tempor incididunt ut labore et dolore magna aliqua. Ut enim ad minim veniam, quis nostrud exercitation ullamco laboris nisi ut aliquip ex ea commodo consequat.

SCOPE OF REPORT:

- Lorem ipsum dolor sit amet, consectetur adipiscing elit, sed do eiusmod tempor incididunt
- ut labore
- et dolore magna aliqua. Ut enim ad minim veniam
- quis nostrud exercitation ullamco laboris nisi ut aliquip ex ea commodo consequat.

REPORT HIGHLIGHTS:

Lorem ipsum dolor sit amet, consectetur adipiscing elit, sed do eiusmod tempor incididunt ut labore et dolore magna aliqua. Ut enim ad minim veniam, quis nostrud exercitation ullamco laboris nisi ut aliquip ex ea commodo consequat. Duis aute irure dolor in reprehenderit in voluptate velit esse cillum dolore eu fugiat nulla pariatur. Excepteur sint occaecat cupidatat non proident, sunt in culpa qui officia deserunt mollit anim id est laborum.

REASONS TO PURCHASE:

- Lorem ipsum dolor sit amet, consectetur adipiscing elit, sed do eiusmod tempor incididunt
- ut labore et dolore magna aliqua. Ut enim ad minim veniam
- quis nostrud exercitation ullamco laboris nisi ut aliquip ex ea commodo consequat
- Duis aute irure dolor in reprehenderit in voluptate velit esse cillum dolore eu

TABLE OF CONTENTS:

View table of contents (opens in a new window)

MARKETING MESSAGE INLUDING CONTACT DETAILS AND/OR EMAIL FORM TO MOTIVATE THE SALE GOES IN HERE.

ADD TO BASKET   **BUY NOW**

Payment Gateways

E-commerce is necessary for online transactions both for the subscription product and for any single-copy report sales. In order to process Credit Card transactions all businesses require a Payment Gateway of some form.

A Payment Gateway is in itself simply a merchant service provided by a software application that interfaces with financial institutions to either authorise, or decline a transaction, based on the key information the end user has submitted.

In Australia, example Payment Gateways include PayPal, Stripe, eWay, SecurePay, Pin Payments. In the UK and/or US the likes of 2Checkout, SagePay, Authorize.net, WorldPay, et cetera. Many more exist and the options are often dictated to you by the bank you are using for your Merchant account, or Merchant Bureau account.

Artificial Intelligence

Artificial intelligence is utilised in the front-end interface to enable users across platforms to access the data sets, individual data item, or specific information as quickly and efficiently as possible.

This functionality enables the platform to operate in a truly conversational manner, effectively enabling each paying client to have a personal Consultant online and at their disposal 24/7.

Additionally, machine learning is used within the platform to personalise the member's content library in order to display the most relevant content.

AI Integrations

Imagine a platform that integrates a job search with audio presentation.

For example, you as a member could ask the platform if there are any Director-level jobs going in Toorak. The platform would then respond back to you and potentially even talk to you about it via your mobile.

Separately, imagine asking the platform what the latest industry news is; or to inform you what the company thinks of the latest product... and then have it read the results back to you using the authors (or curators) own voice, without the author/curator actually speaking the words.

Finally, imagine each member having a personally curated, including all the relevant jobs and news items... that is read to them whenever they wish.

This and a lot more is now possible by implementing the API's below:

Lyrebird AI

Utilising Lyrebird, will enable forward-thinking publishing businesses to transform all content ever written and featured on the website(s) into streaming audio, via podcasts. The beauty of Lyrebird is that you can train it (quickly and easily) to mimic any persons actual voice.

Once you have transformed the content items into natural audio files then you can slice and dice the content to create numerous new products, including job descriptions instantly accessible to the audiences' mobile phones, et alia.

This Montreal-based company is not currently commercial as it is still within the confines of the education sector… and well worth talking to. You might be able to API into them free.

Chatbots

A Chatbot is software which conducts a conversation via auditory or textual methods, often mimicking the behaviour of a human being. Chatbots are built in a similar way as web applications, meaning that the tasks can be divided into design, development and analytics. The Chatbot itself can be cross platform and utilise Email, SMS, messaging and other formats.

Integrate AI-based Chatbot functionality with both the subscription sales funnel; and the support/help desk page. This will increase conversions and (importantly) enable the business to better support overseas subscribers (and potential purchasers.

You should be able to get a rolling free trial for the software if you prepare a script. If not, the subscription is only small making this functionality a no-brainer.

Members of the Board will be able to point you towards the best options here, as they are frequently used in property portals to generate leads for clients.

Google Jobs Discovery Engine

Google is currently in the process of opening up its cloud-based Machine Learning toolkit to jobsite and industry portal developers.

The jobs discovery engine would be an ideal solution to power the search function of the platform.

In-short, Googles Job Discovery engine provides plug and play access to search and machine learning capabilities, enabling the entire recruiting ecosystem – from company job-specific job sites; to horizontal and vertical job boards; and staffing agencies to improve engagement and conversion.

Each portal of our fictional business could integrate this low cost, pay as you go API solution into the platform.

Below is a key list (from Google marketing) that includes the following core functions:

KEYWORD MATCHING – As with traditional search.

COMPANY JARGON RECOGNITION – Understands exactly what a 'Grip' does.

ABBREVIATION RECOGNITION – For example, 'biz dev' = business development.

COMMUTE SEARCH – Shows jobs that are within a 30 minute commute, or near public transportation to the users home location.

SPELLING CORRECTION – This functionality changes the spelling of misspelt words automagically.

CONCEPT RECOGNITION – Understands the difference between lighting and light.

REAL TIME QUERY BROADENING – This increases the scope of the search as per users' preference.

EMPLOYER RECOGNITION – Searching for 'YouTube' returns jobs at YouTube rather than any job with "YouTube" in the description.

JOB ENRICHMENT – Enriching a job with full set of skills

LOCATION MAPPING – Street-level address mapping onto job listings.

LOCATION EXPANSION – Expands on location in the event of no results.

SENIORITY ALIGNMENT – Automatically allocated seniority of a role, which has historically been an issue.

Apps

Despite the fact that our example platform is responsive, it is worth noting that in terms of marketing, apps are notably cheaper to promote than websites.

It is therefore recommended that the business invests in creating apps for the following devices:

→ iPhone
→ Android
→ iPad

Noting much of the functionality we will be talking about, these mobile-friendly apps can be simply skins of the existing website. The key take-home message is, get them listed in the various app stores… and ensure that they work well.

Job Alerts

Offering visitors to the website the ability to be notified of new jobs as and when they are posted is a great way of driving both repeat usage and list building for conversion later.

Job Alerts are typically delivered via the following methods:

- → SMS
- → Messaging and social
- → Toolbars
- → Email

Our example portal business will rely upon Email and social as the primary methods of alerting those registered for the service.

CMS Fundamentals

A content management system (CMS) is a software application that supports the creation and modification of content in the digital environment.

The basic objectives of developing a CMS for the business is to (1) manage content; (2) create content items; and (3) collaborate.

Below is a list of the core features the content management system will include:

POSTING OF ARTICLES – Articles will be able to be posted in real-time to the live site and therefore be added to the content database and not be reliant upon any other technology set-up.

During this process the user will be able to choose the article type within the CMS.

EDITING OF ARTICLES – Articles will be able to be edited using a HTML editor on-board. This can be done at any time within the production lifecycle.

CMS SEARCH – The user will be able to search for relevant articles within the CMS. This will prove useful when adding relevant related links to content.

DELETING OF ARTICLES – Articles will be able to be deleted from the websites via the CMS. Once deleted the articles should not re-appear on the site(s). Again this means breaking the 'bond' with any existing CMS system.

ORDERING OF ARTICLES – The order of articles on the portals should be able to be changed on stated list pages manually. These pages include the homepage, the news homepages and the homepages of any other content type.

The manual ordering of content items potentially increases the editorial value of the portal as the editor can conflate articles together into groupings along the same theme, but outside of the core website taxonomy.

The ordering of the articles on these pages will dictate the content ordering on any newsletter products.

SENDING NEWS ALERTS TO USERS – The ability to send News Alerts to members of the portals will enable the business to automagically market the business to members whenever the portal posts an article on a company and/or subject the end user has subscribed to.

For example a user interested in nanoscience would receive an Email marketing the new article whenever we published one.

CREATING BESPOKE PAGES – Within the CMS designated admin and/or editorial users should be able to create bespoke pages as and when needed. These pages will be allocated the relevant web template, based on the specification.

ABILITY TO PREVIEW ARTICLES – The platforms CMS would allow the Editor to preview the article as it would render on the live site. It would do this by publishing the preview page to the staging server.

ABILITY TO ADD EXTERNAL EVENTS / WEBINARS – This will create a cheap new content source of value to both the end user; and also add to the proposition for corporate subscriptions.

ABILITY TO ADD/EDIT/DELETE WHITE PAPERS AND ADDITIONAL CONTENT – Again, the CMS should enable the user to load, edit, allocate and delete client white papers to individual portals. The white papers themselves should be able to be added to the site for stated periods of time.

This simple functionality will drive usage and also increase revenue opportunities by improving the renewal rate for both Marketing Services clients and the businesses corporate members.

This diagram highlights the fundamental content and functionality of the content delivery platform:

FUNCTIONALITY

CMS	LEAD GENERATION	ENTERPRISE SEARCH	AD SERVER
COMMUNITY	AI	JOBS	SUBSCRIPTIONS
TOOLS	SENTIMENT SCORING	API'S	E-COMMERCE

CONTENT
DELIVERY
PLATFORM

NEWS	BLOGS	COMPANY PROFILES	INDUSTRY PROFILES
COMMENTARY	JOBS	DATA & METRICS	DIARY
VIDEO	STOREFRONTS	DIRECTORY	R&A

CONTENT

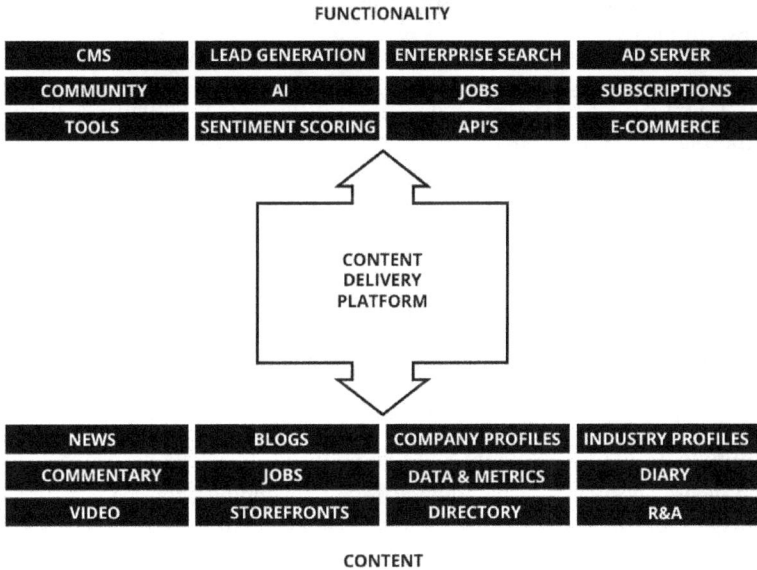

Social Networking Functionality

This section of the book outlines in a list format the functionality included as part of the platforms social networking functionality.

Each feature and function is included to maximize usage of the network and drive the social network areas of the "Conversation Engine".

User Profiles

As this example business has memberships it is vital that those members have profile pages. Pages from which they can establish their identity as part of the industry; and also page from which they can manage the subscription.

MULTI-PART PROFILES – The user profile page is perhaps the most important part of the community functionality. Along with the users profile data, all of the user's content, comments, groups, messages, and statistics can be displayed here.

This page is traditionally used as a point of contact between users, so various options will be available to members (such as "Send Message", "Add to Network" and "Block").

The team tasked with the administration of the network will have the ability to decide what content types go on the users profile pages when and where necessary. This will be different depending upon the precise content makeup of your business.

CUSTOM PROFILE FIELDS – The information that the user provides about themselves will in-turn define the network. Thus, the portal will be able to create profile fields that make users provide information that is relevant to the business.

For example, if we are building a social network for thought leaders aged 18-99 then we would create fields like "Current Employer", "Position", "References", and "Education".

Profile fields will be one of several types: Text fields, pull-down boxes, multi-line text areas, radio buttons, dates, et cetera.

DEPENDENT FIELDS – If we create a pull-down box or radio button profile field during the registration process, or on pages within the property we can give that field one or more dependent profile fields.

This functionality can be used across the platform.

KEYWORD LINKS – If enabled, some of the profile fields on the portal will be "linked, separated by commas." In-short, this means that whatever data the individual member provides in these fields will be separated by commas and linked to browse pages.

For example, if we were to have a field called "Favourite subjects" and a member enters "nanoscience, scale, Fullerenes ", each of those words will be linked on the user's profile page. Then, when a viewer clicks "nanoscience", they are taken to a page that lists all other users that have listed "nanoscience" in their "Favourite subjects" field.

PHOTOS AND AVATARS – Members of the portals should be able to upload a picture of themselves, which is then automagically sized down and used as their profile avatar, perhaps using ImageMajick, or something similar. This is also displayed in search results, when they comment, send a message, and across the network as a whole.

SUBSCRIPTION MANAGEMENT – Members can check and amend their subscription status and payment details at any time quickly and easily.

PROFILE PRIVACY – Members of the portals can select from several privacy levels when managing their account.

Network Structure & Customizability

SUB-NETWORKS – The platforms social network will have the ability to organize its users into "sub-networks" based on profile information they have in common with each other.

Platform administrators can use this to limit access and privacy between sub-networks, display sub-network-specific content in the page templates, or to simply organize your users.

For example, we might want the social network to be comprised of two sub-networks: "Scientists" and "Management". Or, perhaps you might want to split these up into "Scientists in Melbourne", "Scientists outside Melbourne", "Management in Australia", and "Management outside Australia".

This is particularly useful because at a later date the platform can show different content (or advertisements) to users based on what sub-network they are in. This allows the business to serve them information or ads that are specifically relevant to their interests or personal characteristics.

Great for increasing the relevance... and therefore response rate of adverts.

SEVERAL RELATIONSHIP STRUCTURES – The network can select from four distinct friendship structures:

- → Nobody can invite anyone to become friends.
- → Anybody can invite anyone to become friends.
- → Only people within the same sub-network can become friends.
- → Users can only invite their friends' friends (second-level friends) to become their friends.

ONE-WAY OR TWO-WAY RELATIONSHIPS – As the admin, the Producers can decide if users have one-way or two-way friendships.

For example: User 1 adds User 2 to his, or her friend list. With a one-way friendship framework, User 2 is now User 1's friend, but User 1 is not User 2's pal. With a two-way friendship framework, User 2 is User 1's friend and User 1 is User 2's friend.

VERIFIED OR UNVERIFIED RELATIONSHIPS – The business can choose whether or not users will have to confirm friendship requests.

For example: User 1 requests to become friends with User 2. With a verified friendships framework, the two users will not become friends until User 2 confirms the friendship.

RELATIONSHIP TYPES (TITLES) – The platform can create a list of friendship types for users to pick when describing their relationships with their friends.

For example: The friendship type list may be something like "Colleague", "Client", "Friend", "Manager", and so on. Individual members can pick from these from drop-down boxes when they add new friends or edit the details of their network.

RELATIONSHIP EXPLANATIONS – The platform allows members to type in a brief explanation of their relationships.

PUBLIC / PRIVATE SECTIONS – Portal administrators will be able to make portions of the community available to the public or to registered users only.

This enables the business to potentially have roundtables and/or focus groups by invite only, controlled discussions and to potentially plug in webinars and offline events into the network.

CUSTOM PRIVACY – The business can decide what privacy levels our users can choose from when they decide who can view (or post comments on) their profiles.

SIGN-UP BY ADMIN INVITATION – The business can choose to allow users to sign-up only if we have invited them. This is an effective way to build an exclusive controlled community, or roundtable.

SIGN-UP BY USER INVITATION – Portal administrators can allow members to sign-up only if they have been invited by an existing member.

The business can even give each member a limited number of invitations to send out. By limiting sign-ups in this way, invitations can become "valuable," which is a known method of achieving viral growth.

EMAIL MESSAGES – The social network sends Emails to its users when they do different things, like sign-up, receive friend requests, request their lost password, et cetera. These Email messages should be 100 per cent customisable.

~~~~~~

Look & Feel

TEMPLATE ENGINE – This allows members of the portal to control the look and feel of their profile. Every single page of the network should have a HTML template that the user can modify.

Using special tags, the site could display virtually any information from our databases on any part of your network.

PORTAL PAGE – This is the homepage for the platforms community. It should feature a map of users around the world that are online.

The homepage should also feature content from the "Conversation Engine".

GOOGLE MAPS – Show each individual member's location with an embedded Google Map on their profile.

Members can also search by location, visualizing your member's locations on a single large map.

In addition to the Google Map on the users profile page a Google Map featuring the geo-location of all users appears on the homepage... and a

Google Map showing those participating in individual debates also features.

Anti-spam Features

EMAIL ADDRESS VERIFICATION – The business can choose to force users to verify their Email address (by clicking a link that arrives in an Email after they sign-up) before they can login to their account.

This is an effective way of reducing fake (automated) account sign-ups and spam on the platform.

RANDOM PASSWORD GENERATOR – The business can choose to have a random password Emailed to each user that signs up, enhancing the security of their account, verifying their Email address, and increasing the probability that they are human and not an automated program.

CAPTCHA IMAGES – When folk sign-up, we can force them to visually read the alphanumeric code from an automatically generated image and enter it into a field. This feature reduces spam and automated sign-ups. It can be used on several areas of the social network, including sign-up and comments.

INAPPROPRIATE CONTENT REPORTS – Users can submit an inappropriate content report if they consider an image (or any other content) to be offensive or spam-related. These reports can be managed by the admin team.

SIMPLE USER MANAGEMENT – The admin panel within the platforms CMS will include an easy-to-use interface for managing (and deleting) users, content items, groups, et cetera, allowing the portal administrator to easily delete poor quality, or SPAM content.

~~~~~~

Blogs

WYSIWYG COMPOSER – Users compose their blog entries with ease using an embedded, rich text MSWord styled editor. With one click, users can view the HTML source of their entry and make changes if necessary.

BLOG ENTRY CATEGORIES – The business can create an unlimited number of blog entry categories. When writing their blog entries, members can specify what category they belong to.

This is a useful feature, particularly if you want to create a page that displays all of the blog entries on the social network that are about.

Great for the "Conversation Engine" functionality.

BLOG ENTRY PRIVACY – Members of the network can select from several levels of privacy when deciding who can view and comment on their blog entries.

~~~~~~

Interest Groups

CUSTOMIZABLE GROUP FIELDS – When members create a new group on the platform, they are asked to provide some information and details about it.

These fields can be any of several types, including text fields, pull-down boxes, multi-line text areas, dates, companies, and so forth.

GROUP CATEGORIES – The business may want to allow your users to categorize their groups by subject, location, et cetera.

Categorized groups make it easier for users to find and join groups that interest them. We can create an unlimited number of group categories and subcategories.

BROWSE GROUPS – Users can browse groups by category or search for groups by keyword. This makes it easy for them to find and join groups and in-turn conversations that interest them.

GROUP FILE LIBRARY – Each group is given its own unique file library, where PDF and other approved file types can be loaded.

MEMBERSHIP RANKINGS – Groups within the community can contain three levels of membership: Leadership, Officer, and Member.

When a subscriber creates a group, they are automatically made the leader of that group; and a link is then included on the users homepage, thus allowing easy access for the subscriber.

Leadership can be transferred to another user if desired. Leaders can also appoint officers, who have limited administration abilities such as approving/rejecting new members, changing the group settings, and so forth.

Members can view the group's content, but cannot alter its settings.

MEMBERSHIP APPROVAL – Groups can be set to "allow new members by approval only", as you currently see on some LinkedIn Groups. This means that when a prospective new member requests to join the group, they must first be approved by the group leader or admin.

MEMBERSHIP INVITATIONS - Group leaders can send invitations to other users to become members of their group. If they so choose, members are notified by Email when they receive an invitation. This is especially useful should an education establishment, or business want to set a group up on the portal.

GROUP DISCUSSION BOARD – Each group includes a discussion board, allowing members to post threaded discussion topics. These sit outside of the conversation engine.

Private Messages

MAILBOXES – Users are supplied with a webmail-style message manager where they can view both incoming and outgoing private messages.

MESSAGE LIMITS – The business can decide how many messages each user is able to store in their inbox/outbox.

NEW MESSAGE NOTIFICATIONS – Portal members can choose to receive Email notifications each time they receive a private message. This encourages interactivity and return visits to your social network.

Browse/Search

SEPARATE SQL DATABASE (for scalability) – The integrated search engine stores its data in a separate SQL database. If the network grows to be very large, we can move this database to another server to save resources and reduce server load.

IMMEDIATE INDEXING – Every time a user updates their profile, uploads something to their album, writes a blog entry, et cetera, the search engine's cache of the page they modified is updated. This means that pages indexed by the search engine will be searchable on a "near real-time" basis.

Other Tools

EMAIL ANNOUNCEMENTS – Through the admin panel, you can compose and send an Email to every user on your system. This is an effective way to encourage inactive users to return to your social network.

SITE ANNOUNCEMENTS – Through the admin panel, the portals admin team can post news announcements.

COMPREHENSIVE STATISTICS – The admin panel includes a social network statistics area. This area features automatically-generated graphs that show you the levels of activity on your social network over various time periods.

ACCESS LOG – The admin panel will include a list of the last 100, or so login attempts to the network. This gives us an effective way of identifying and banning/controlling usage from abusive users.

User Polls

POLL CREATION – The poll creation function allows our users to create and share polls with other users on their individual profile pages. It will add another usage generating activity to the network.

BROWSE FUNCTIONALITY – Members will also be able to search for polls via a "browse polls" area, and each users' own polls will appear on their profile and recent activity feed.

The polls will be navigable by date and be arranged in a way similar to that of the Daily Mails polls.

Address Book Importing

If you have a community, having the ability to allow users to import their contact data is key to growing the network. LinkedIn and most large-scale networks utilise ActiveX (for Outlook) and webmail-based (Gmail, Yahoo, et al) address book imports.

Additionally, social network imports are also an attractive proposition.

By allowing members to importing their address books you are enabling them to promote the website for you. These names will act as a lead generation mechanism for the business.

The ability to import an address book of a user during the sign-up process is vital to the growth of the network.

It is arguable to say that no social network would have ever achieved critical mass without this core, yet often overlooked or poorly implemented functionality.

I would recommend that the platform integrate a webmail-based address book importing system into the registration process. –Make it optional at the very end of the process.

To utilise the functionality, I would integrate the registration process on the platform with a service called CloudSponge.

Additional Functionality

This list of additional desirable functionalities primarily concentrated on ideas and content relating to recruitment portions of the websites. Most, if not all are suitable for any industry, or job function specific properties.

CAREER TESTS

➜ Psychometric test (Scientific)
➜ Job suitability test

SALARY CALCULATORS – Wizard-like functionality that uses data based on region, industry and job title to predict how much an individual should be earning.

➜ Benchmark and compare your salary to others

CAREER MATCHING WIZARD – Functionality that enables the user to match his/her qualifications, experience and interest areas to individual jobs and/or industries.

CAREER PLANNING WIZARD – This functionality enables the user to plan their long-term career.

CV LIBRARY – Allows the users of the site to load and save their CV to their profile.

CV BROADCASTING SERVICE – Enable the user to send their resume to a number of agencies relevant to the members' desired and/or actual location and industry. Agencies could opt-in to the service.

CONTRACTOR PRICE CALCULATOR – An interactive guide (and calculator) that enables the user to put a cost next to the skill-set required.

By adding the number of contractors.

SALARY SURVEY BROWSER – This functionality enables subscribers to browse data from the latest salary survey and compare with previous surveys. As the portals age, the importance of this grows. Functionality based around prognosticating the future salary of roles could also be included. In order to achieve this you would need two years data, plus whatever the local inflation rate is.

CHAPTER 7

Content Strategy

Historically, producing content has proven to be an expensive business.

The strategy outlined in this part of the document utilises modern content types; introduces a reliable industry voice to the user proposition; next generation content creation practices, such as automation, slicing and dicing, AI and digitalisation; and (importantly) a new more scalable content model.

Raison d'etre

Defining the purpose of the business is one of the key steps to understanding both why a company exists; and in the case of content to creating the right type of content to meet this purpose.

The content featured across the network should therefore be driven by this purpose.

Voice and Tone

The voice and tone on the platform establishes the credibility of the vision, purpose, and positioning through communication. This once mixed with the visual identity of the websites in-turn becomes *the brand*.

Please note that the example below is set to meet the expectation of the audience. These will need to be worked on in order to fit whatever audience you are trying to hit. In this case the business is in the emerging technology space.

Example

From an editorial perspective, every item of content written should be seen as:

INTERESTING – The author and publisher just told me something I was not aware of.

BOLD – The author and publisher are unafraid.

PERSONAL – The business writers are like me. I can relate to them.

PROUD – The business is a great company supporting our industry.

THOUGHTFUL – The author and business has clearly thought a lot about the issue. They are thought leaders.

INSIGHTFUL – The portal offers significant value to members.

TRUTHFUL – The business tells its readers the truth, as it sees it.

These simple rules form the basis of much of an editorial direction document.

Key Priorities for B2B Content Producers

The table below highlights the results from a survey undertaken by the Content Marketing Institute. As you can immediately see, producers are looking to create better engagement; to understand what is working for them; and to repurpose existing content.

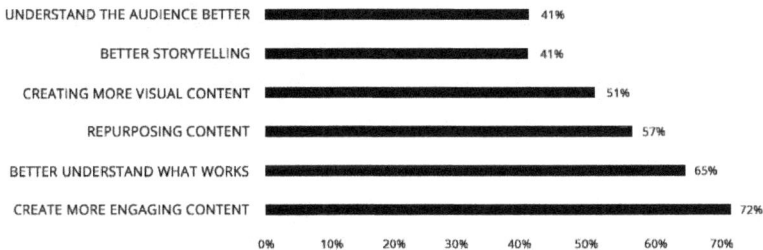

Priority	Percentage
UNDERSTAND THE AUDIENCE BETTER	41%
BETTER STORYTELLING	41%
CREATING MORE VISUAL CONTENT	51%
REPURPOSING CONTENT	57%
BETTER UNDERSTAND WHAT WORKS	65%
CREATE MORE ENGAGING CONTENT	72%

Example Content Types

Below is a list of content types a member-based property like our example network could be including in its proposition:

→ Job listings
→ Company news
→ Action plans
→ Interviews

- → Product news
- → Industry news
- → R&D news
- → How to's
- → Membership calls
- → Q&A's
- → Webinars
- → Video
- → Daily vlog
- → Blogs
- → Advice articles
- → Commentary
- → Downloads
- → Free reports
- → Live blogs
- → Podcasts
- → User profiles
- → Company profiles
- → Industry profiles
- → Data sets
- → Courses
- → Cheat sheets
- → Workbooks
- → Knowledgebase
- → Meet-ups
- → Events
- → SaaS/tools
- → Services
- → Photo galleries
- → Careers
- → Illustrations
- → Case studies
- → Infographics
- → Storefronts
- → Archives
- → Website news
- → Perks
- → eBooks
- → Education
- → Discussions
- → Forums
- → Research
- → Metrics
- → Polls
- → Glossary
- → Guides
- → Competitions

Choosing the Correct Content

The type of content that works best for a platform depends very much upon the audience expectation and industry requirement.

For example, a vertical industry platform aimed at the screen arts would likely want to feature reviews of movies and television either from a technical standpoint, or on an artistic basis.

The example business outlined in this book covers the emerging technology space so has an entirely different requirement.

Take time to think about the precise challenges professionals within your target industry face.

The Chosen Content Types

Below is an outline of each emerging technology portals specification, complete with a brief description and specification of the content sets:

PRODUCT NEWS – The latest news relating to product/services within the target vertical. This kind of content can be sourced from corporate press releases and care should be taken to ensure that the article is more than 350 words in length, but also is rewritten.

The content manager needs to be vigilant with this, especially if the content is produced offshore.

COMPANY NEWS – Corporate news and filings. Again, this can be sourced from corporate press releases and newswires. When writing each entry should be checked for uniqueness.

Each entry should have some level of commentary about it so that it has some content. Context and commentary are key.

INDUSTRY NEWS – News that relates to either the industry as a whole, or from education establishments. These articles are of relatively high value and should be longer in length and offer significant value to the reader.

For our example business, this is perhaps the most important content as it centres the portals on the industry they are covering.

R&D NEWS – The latest industry research and development news from the education and foundation space. This kind of content is important to the portals as it highlights the direction the industry is travelling. The subjects themselves can be sourced from academia, from PhD papers, interviews and press releases.

COLLATED NEWS / BLOG – News collated by the editor and sourced from around the web. This is a commentary on other sources news. The content acts as a round-up from external sources and ensures that the portal does not miss anything significant within the industry.

INDUSTRY PROFILES – In-depth profiles of the industry vertical, broken down by country, region or as a whole. The reports will feature market size and key fundamentals for the industry.

Each of the initial thirty (30) Industry Profiles, broken down by country and/or region will be created for $300 by an offshore content partner prior to launch. This will support the subscription-based content set of the portals.

COMPANY PROFILES, INCLUDING SWOT'S – A profile of all companies operating within the sector. Each company profile features an overview of the business, history, products and services, subsidiaries, financial performance and a SWOT analysis.

Initially, each SWOT analysis will be produced on-demand by an in-house team, with a 48 hour turnaround time.

Each Company Profile, excluding the SWOT analysis would be unique created via a content partner for $200.

An estimated 200 company profiles will be acquired prior to launch in order to support the subscription-based content set of each individual portal.

RESEARCH STORE – Buy research reports via the report store. The report store features not only self-branded reports, but also third-party reports provided by generalist R&A providers.

The business will take a revenue share of each report purchased via the store. The revenue share percentage can vary between 50-70 per cent to the producer, depending upon negotiation.

KNOWLEDGE BASE – Produced in article format, this section features portions of reports and research data sourced from our platform that each portal release to the greater industry.

This content will include tables and metrics and is of high importance to the proposition.

DEALS DATABASE – An updated daily feed of all the latest R&A news and deals within the sector. This content type is simply a reuse of existing Company News content and could be programmatically managed and displayed by company, by date and by taxonomy in a dashboard format.

GLOSSARY – A collection of acronyms and words designed to act as a reference for registered users.

Personally, I like glossary content as it enables the end user to learn 'on the fly' without mistaking definitions. This is one of the reasons why I have included a glossary within this book.

JOB BOARD – International in scope, the job board features all job listings relevant to the sector. Posting to the board is initially offered for free, but with plans to charge at a later date.

Each job posting should try to be unique. This is obviously difficult as recruiters often post jobs using an XML-based feed. However, the fact remains, the more original jobs-based content appearing on the property the better.

COMMUNITY – Account and subscription management functionality for all registered users. This also enables paid users to market themselves effectively to the network by allowing threaded messages, discussions and more.

COURSE FINDER – A search-based facility listing all the latest degree, post-graduate and professional qualifications from around the world relating to the vertical.

SUPPLIERS DIRECTORY – Marketing profiles of businesses that supply the vertical. These storefronts enable suppliers to advertise the products/services they offer to the resident audience.

DAILY NEWSLETTERS – A daily summary of all that happened the previous day in the sector.

DIARY – This is a weekly 'what's on' guide to the industry. –This is an often overlooked form of strategic content. As a result this content would not only be published in textual format, but should also be within a weekly video production.

EDUCATION DATABASE – This is relatively easy structured content to produce as all it takes to compile is a list of University establishments; the industry-relevant courses they offer; and specific details.

An Example Content Matrix

The following table outlines the individual content types and user access permissions:

	ARTIFICIAL INTELLIGENCE	INDUSTRY COMMENTARY	INDUSTRY METRICS	COLLATED NEWS / BLOG	PRODUCT NEWS	COMPANY NEWS	INDUSTRY NEWS	R&D NEWS	DEALS DATABASE	SUPPLIERS STOREFRONTS	COMMUNITY	EDUCATION DATABASE	SALARY SURVEY	JOB LISTINGS	EXT RESEARCH REPORTS	RECRUITMENT TIPS	COMPANY PROFILES	INDUSTRY PROFILES	QTR UPDATE REPORTS	MANAGEMENT REPORTS	DAILY NEWSLETTERS
VIRTUAL REALITY																					
FREE	NO	LTD 3	NO	X	LTD 3	LTD 3	LTD 3	LTD 3	NO	X	LTD 3	NO	NO	NO	$$$	LTD 3	NO	NO	$$$	$$$	NO
REGISTERED USER	NO	LTD 6	LTD 6	X	LTD 6	LTD 6	LTD 6	LTD 6	NO	X	LTD 6	X	NO	X	$$$	X	NO	NO	$$$	$$$	X
INDIVIDUAL MEMBERSHIP	X	X	X	X	X	X	X	X	NO	X	X	X	X	X	$$$	X	X	X	$$$	$$$	X
CORPORATE MEMBER	X	X	X	X	X	X	X	X	X	X	X	X	X	X	$$$	X	X	X	$$$	$$$	X
SPACE TECHNOLOGY																					
FREE	NO	LTD 3	NO	X	LTD 3	LTD 3	LTD 3	LTD 3	NO	X	LTD 3	NO	NO	NO	$$$	LTD 3	NO	NO	$$$	$$$	NO
REGISTERED USER	NO	LTD 6	LTD 6	X	LTD 6	LTD 6	LTD 6	LTD 6	NO	X	LTD 6	X	NO	X	$$$	X	NO	NO	$$$	$$$	X
INDIVIDUAL MEMBERSHIP	X	X	X	X	X	X	X	X	NO	X	X	X	X	X	$$$	X	X	X	$$$	$$$	X
CORPORATE MEMBER	X	X	X	X	X	X	X	X	X	X	X	X	X	X	$$$	X	X	X	$$$	$$$	X
GENOMICS																					
FREE	NO	LTD 3	NO	X	LTD 3	LTD 3	LTD 3	LTD 3	NO	X	LTD 3	NO	NO	NO	$$$	LTD 3	NO	NO	$$$	$$$	NO
REGISTERED USER	NO	LTD 6	LTD 6	X	LTD 6	LTD 6	LTD 6	LTD 6	NO	X	LTD 6	X	NO	X	$$$	X	NO	NO	$$$	$$$	X
INDIVIDUAL MEMBERSHIP	NO	X	X	X	X	X	X	X	NO	X	X	X	X	X	$$$	X	X	X	$$$	$$$	X
CORPORATE MEMBER	X	X	X	X	X	X	X	X	X	X	X	X	X	X	$$$	X	X	X	$$$	$$$	X
ARTIFICIAL INTELLIGENCE																					
FREE	NO	LTD 3	NO	X	LTD 3	LTD 3	LTD 3	LTD 3	NO	X	LTD 3	NO	NO	NO	$$$	LTD 3	NO	NO	$$$	$$$	NO
REGISTERED USER	NO	LTD 6	LTD 6	X	LTD 6	LTD 6	LTD 6	LTD 6	NO	X	LTD 6	X	NO	X	$$$	X	NO	X	$$$	$$$	X
INDIVIDUAL MEMBERSHIP	X	X	X	X	X	X	X	X	NO	X	X	X	X	X	$$$	X	X	X	$$$	$$$	X
CORPORATE MEMBER	X	X	X	X	X	X	X	X	X	X	X	X	X	X	$$$	X	X	X	$$$	$$$	X
ALTERNATIVE ENERGY																					
FREE	NO	LTD 3	NO	X	LTD 3	LTD 3	LTD 3	LTD 3	NO	X	LTD 3	NO	NO	NO	$$$	LTD 3	NO	NO	$$$	$$$	NO
REGISTERED USER	NO	LTD 6	LTD 6	X	LTD 6	LTD 6	LTD 6	LTD 6	NO	X	LTD 6	X	NO	X	$$$	X	NO	X	$$$	$$$	X
INDIVIDUAL MEMBERSHIP	X	X	X	X	X	X	X	X	NO	X	X	X	X	X	$$$	X	X	X	$$$	$$$	X
CORPORATE MEMBER	X	X	X	X	X	X	X	X	X	X	X	X	X	X	$$$	X	X	X	$$$	$$$	X
NANOTECHNOLOGY																					
FREE	NO	LTD 3	NO	X	LTD 3	LTD 3	LTD 3	LTD 3	NO	X	LTD 3	NO	NO	NO	$$$	LTD 3	NO	NO	$$$	$$$	NO
REGISTERED USER	NO	LTD 6	LTD 6	X	LTD 6	LTD 6	LTD 6	LTD 6	NO	X	LTD 6	X	NO	X	$$$	X	NO	NO	$$$	$$$	X
INDIVIDUAL MEMBERSHIP	X	X	X	X	X	X	X	X	NO	X	X	X	X	X	$$$	X	X	X	$$$	$$$	X
CORPORATE MEMBER	X	X	X	X	X	X	X	X	X	X	X	X	X	X	$$$	X	X	X	$$$	$$$	X
PHARMA TECHNOLOGY																					
FREE	NO	LTD 3	NO	X	LTD 3	LTD 3	LTD 3	LTD 3	NO	X	LTD 3	NO	NO	NO	$$$	LTD 3	NO	NO	$$$	$$$	NO
REGISTERED USER	NO	LTD 6	LTD 6	X	LTD 6	LTD 6	LTD 6	LTD 6	NO	X	LTD 6	X	NO	X	$$$	X	NO	NO	$$$	$$$	X
INDIVIDUAL MEMBERSHIP	X	X	X	X	X	X	X	X	NO	X	X	X	X	X	$$$	X	X	X	$$$	$$$	X
CORPORATE MEMBER	X	X	X	X	X	X	X	X	X	X	X	X	X	X	$$$	X	X	X	$$$	$$$	X

Covering the Bases

Evergreen content is best defined as content that is always relevant to the end user.

This kind of content is perhaps the most important content on the website both in terms of SEO and also in terms garnering gravitas and respect for the product amongst the target audience. It enables the property to 'cover the bases' and achieve a degree of relevance to the industry professional that would be impossible without the content.

It is therefore highly recommended that some time and attention is paid to getting the best quality of content possible.

A couple of examples are used within this document highlighting 'evergreen' content for the nanotechnology sector.

Below is an additional list of content that could be produced:

➜ Research-based content
➜ Industry analysis, Porters 5 forces, et alia
➜ Competitive intelligence articles such as a SWOT analysis
➜ Individual metrics and statistics relating to the sector
➜ Checklists
➜ Cheat sheets
➜ Top 10's and resource lists
➜ How to guides
➜ Career advice
➜ Best practice documents
➜ Reviews
➜ Glossary of terms
➜ White papers
➜ Case studies
➜ Industry timelines
➜ Infographics
➜ Databases

Example Evergreen Content

This section of the book features some examples of evergreen content. The examples have been produced for our fictional nanotechnology portal.

Introduction to Nanotechnology

In the early 1980's, American engineer Eric Drexler introduced the idea of creating a technology at the molecular scale to be used across all levels of science. Speaking in terms of nanometres, hence the industry name, his vision included designing motors, robotic limbs and even whole computers at a size so small, they could easily fit inside a singular cell.

Over the next decade, Drexler spent enormous time and energy to render the possibility of nanotechnology an acceptable concept within the scientific community. As this seemingly fictional idea was further developed, technological advances were simultaneously being made that would allow engineers to build basic structures at a molecular degree (CRN).

The original meaning of nanotechnology refers to constructing machines of any type from the ground up with molecular precision, and idea already proposed in 1959 by Nobel Prize recipient Richard Feynman.

Considered the father of nanotechnology, Feynman was a renowned physicist who described a process in his speech entitled "There's Plenty of Room at the Bottom" in which scientists would have the ability to influence and restrain individual atoms and molecules for a specific and intended purpose (Nano.gov). It was that notion that inspired the nanoscience industry and the birth of a new technological revolution.

To better understand the idea of the scale engineers are working with, take a newspaper for example. One sheet of newspaper is approximately 100,000 nanometres thick. Zoom in a little further, and presume one nanometre is the size of a marble. That would render the entire Earth merely a meter in length.

Generally, nanotechnology machines are constructed to the size of 100 nanometres or smaller (Economy Watch). Across the world, there are currently over 1,000 examples of this technology in use in a multitude of industries.

The innovation and precision of nanotech breakthroughs have significantly restructured the markets in the manufacturing, biotechnology, environmental and pharmaceutical industries.

According to BBC Research, and industry leader in science and technology market study, the efficiency of nanotechnologies has significantly enhanced market demand for global applications of technology (BBC Research). And as with any industry, the huge driver for this development is the one factor that all businesses around the globe understand: money.

Whilst nanotechnology is exciting and incites curiosity at its unfathomed possibilities, customer demand today calls for faster, smaller and cheaper (Adams and Rogers).

Helping to revolutionize many industry sectors, nanotech devices can be found in information technology, energy, environmental science, medicine, homeland security, food safety, transportation and many others.

Materials can be made lighter, stronger, more durable, and more effective with the enhancements of nanoscience.

For example, nanoscale additives to composite materials provide lightweight ballistic deflection in military body armour. Also, nanocomposites in food containers can reduce the growth of bacteria, rendering foods fresher and safer for longer periods of time.

Nanotechnology is contributing to the development of cleaner, renewable energy sources such as converting cellulose into ethanol for fuel (Nano.gov).

Most conspicuously, nanotechnology is starring as the innovation with the most potential to revolutionize the medical field. Nano-based products have been developed to serve as contrast agents in cell imaging, improving accuracy while reducing costs of care (Nanotech Industries).

Furthermore, this technology has been successful in early detection of degenerative diseases and has also shown great promise for detecting the rare molecular signals associated with cell malignancy.

In other words, nanoscale components may soon be able to detect cancerous cells and direct treatment at a much earlier stage, preventing further spread (Nano.gov).

There is an unprecedented level of reach that the nanotechnology industry can impact, with extraordinary potential to evolve the world's understanding of science.

In the words of Nobel Prize winner Dr Horst Störmer,

"...it's not until we start putting atoms together that we can make anything useful."

Introduction to the Nanoscale

Since the mid-1980's, the topic of molecular science has branched out. One particular aspect is the development of the nanoscale, also known as the nanoscopic scale.

In recent years, researchers have discovered that atomic particles can not only be manipulated, but they can be controlled for particular uses in technology.

Working at the nanoscale level means more than designing technology in much smaller dimensions; it enables scientists to create structures by employing materials at the atomic level, capitalizing the specific chemical and mechanical properties in their naturally occurring state.

As precise as the science of nanotechnology is, it is vital to understand resources at the nanoscale in order to manipulate those materials at an exact level for them to be useful.

To illustrate how miniscule the nanoscale is, take a raindrop for example. The aver-age large raindrop is approximately 2.5 millimetres in diameter. The prefix 'milli' references a factor of one thousandth. In comparison, the prefix 'nano' references a factor one billionth. That raindrop diameter is equivalent to 2,500,000 nanometres.

The difference in scale is astronomical. A common biological element in genetic science revolves around DNA. One strand of human DNA is measured at approximately 2.5 nanometres wide (US National Nanotechnology Initiative, 2015).

The importance of understanding this scale and how to apply it for advances in nanoscience lies in the properties of particles at this level. When solid matter is viewed under a standard optical microscope, there aren't many differences in the physical or functional characteristics, if any at all.

However, when viewed at the nanoscale level, these observed properties differ in quantum effects and behaviours, and thus are able to be applied in new ways.

Some of those differences are evidenced in changes to melting point, fluorescence, magnetic permeability, chemical reactivity and electrical conductivity (US National Nano-technology Initiative, 2015). These property differences open up a whole new territory for particles to be used.

Nanoscale technology is the realm where otherwise diverse fields, such as engineering, biology, physics and chemistry converge. This level provides the key for manipulating special properties to discover new and innovative uses for materials.

The first known example of this technology was exhibited on November 11, 1989, when a team of researchers at IBM were able to move xenon atoms on a background of copper atoms to spell out the company name (US National Nanotechnology Initiative, 2015).

Today, scientists are using this ability to create materials at the nanoscale for medical devices and drugs that cure diseases at the molecular level. Advances are also being made in other industries, such as energy efficiency developments in composite structures that use less fuel.

Furthering this technology, scientists are drawing on the nanoscale of biology to design new tools and treatments that will be more precise and tailored to individuals.

The bio-barcode assay, for example, is a low-cost technique used to detect biomarkers specific to a disease in blood samples. Through various testing, this process has proven to be significantly more effective than other conventional assays for targeted biomarkers (US National Nanotechnology Initiative, 2015).

The science that allowed this technology to be developed is directly associated with the understanding of particles and their properties on the nanoscale.

Engineering and medical industries aren't the only fields benefiting from the study and advances in nanoscale science.

The cosmetic industry is already using nanoscale titanium dioxide and zine oxide in an unconsolidated, powder form for facial creams and sunscreen lotion. These particles also have use for their reflective properties in paint.

Cutting tools have been coated with a nanostructured wear-resistant covering. Even US naval vessels are incorporating nanotechnology in applications to increase durability (Committee for the Review of the National Nanotechnology Initiative, 2002).

The field of information technology is one of the prime beneficiaries of nanoscale research and developments. And much of the near-term advances are showing potential to thrust that progress even further.

Nanotechnology will improve cost structures and performance standards of products in the industry, such as faster transistors and silicon microelectronic chips capable of higher storage capacity.

Even more, advances in photonic crystals are closing the gap for optical networks and allowing the full potential of multiplexing to be realized (Committee for the Review of the National Nanotechnology Initiative, 2002).

Nanoscale science seeks to create new materials with significantly different proper-ties than their larger scale counterparts for new uses in a variety of fields. There are many potential applications for nanotechnology that show great promise in revolutionizing the world.

Current developments are already impacting the US economy and market infrastructure with advances developed enough to assure future impacts. From biological molecule detectors to quantum computers, industries all around are benefiting from nanoscale science.

Nanotechnology Timeline

Whilst often seen as something for the future, nanotechnology has already revolutionised the world we live in. It continues to pass through an evolutionary process as our knowledge and understanding increase; and our technical abilities expand.

Below is a brief primer relating to the historical development of nanotechnology ranging from more than 1,000 years ago, through the 18th and 19th centuries, right up until the new millennium.

PRE-MODERN EXAMPLES OF NANOTECHNOLOGY

Though there are many large-scale monuments and works of great art created in ancient times like the pyramids on the Giza plateau, Macchu Picchu in the Andes and the Great Wall of China, mathematicians, and even artisans of that period were also skilled in the Nano scale.

Generally it is thought that the controlling and adaptation of matter at the Nano scale is a recent achievement, craftsmen in the past were also adept at using material at the tiniest scales.

Nanotechnology has revolutionized the modern world. It has passed through an evolutionary process. Nanotechnology was advancing mankind back then in a similar, if less pronounced way than it is advancing humanity today. It developed and has continued to develop in successive evolutionary stages.

The history of nanotechnology can be traced in the fourth century. Lycurgus Cup can be cited as its classical example during that time period; a stunning use of nanoscience by the Romans. It is an example of the dichroic glass: a combination of silver and gold in the glass. When it is lit from outside it look dull, green and glowing red from inside.

Similarly, Maya Blue, an azure pigment to resist corrosion was produced in 800AD which was discovered in the Mayan city of Chichen Itza. It contained clay along Nano-pores combined with indigo dye. It was used to create stable pigment of the environment.

Moreover, when we move little further, nanotechnology can be seen in little modern form. In the sixth century, vibrant stained glass windows were the example of the nanotechnology. Nano-particles of gold chloride give colours to these glass windows along with some particles of chlorides and metal oxides.

These glass windows were used to purify the air as these Nano-particles worked as photo-catalytic. Sun rays were used to activate these Nano-particles to destroy the pollutants in the air. The process of cleaning air from pollutant was done in a pretty much sophisticated way as glass windows worked in the presence of the sun rays. Ceramics from over the "Renaissance Mediterranean" world was frequently enlivened with a brilliant metallic coating called gloss; Nano-particles of silver and copper were used to give appropriate colour and shine.

However, according to the Ian Freestone, early artisans could not be regarded as scientists as they were not aware of the fact that they were actually working in the nanoscale. Peter Paufler termed the early development of nanotechnology as evolution as that of biological evolution.

In the 9th century the evolutionary process of nanotechnology moved a step further in shape of translucent, glittering ceramic glazes. These ceramic glazes were used by the Muslims. Early Muslims scientists contributed much in the development of nanotechnology.

In the 13th century Damascus was the fort of knowledge, people from all around the world used to travel to Damascus to acquire knowledge. In this era Saber Blades garnered a high reputation. These Blades were made of carbon nanotubes along with wire of cementite. It was use to hold a sharp edge which added strength by carbon steel formulation.

These early developments of the nanotechnology were a result of the trial and error and experiments done over hundred years. Knowledge was passed from generation to generation along with improvements in it till the time it reached in modern times.

NANOTECHNOLOGY IN THE MODERN ERA

In the 19th century, nanotechnology was quite developed and well thought out as a scientist at that time were using some sophisticated scientific techniques to explore the potential of matter at Nano level. However, early developments of the 19th century cannot be regarded as sophisticated as they are today.

An early example of nanotechnology is photography. Light sensitive silver Nano-particles were used to produce those photographs. Although attempts were made to produce such photographs by some scientists as Thomas Wedgewood and Sir Humphry, but their photographs were temporal and could not last for longer time.

However in, 1827, a successful attempt was made by Joseph Niepce. He used such materials which were hardened if exposed to the light. Almost eight hours of light were required to these pictures. Latter his works were carried out by his partner Louis Daguerre, who in 1839 was able to produce photographic plates reducing the time of light exposure.

With the passage of time, the field of science developed immensely in all aspects including understanding of science, instrumentation and experimentation. It was because of this understanding of the sophisticated scientific instrumentation and experimentation, that it became possible to study Nano-particles.

Scientists have conducted several studies and successfully studied these particles, giving rise to new developments, by utilizing the knowledge, learned from the experiences; it was found that Nano-size particles of gold can give coloured liquids when provided with some certain light conditions.

The work that was carried out during the mid – 1900's was revolutionizing in the field of engineering and technology and it laid the foundations of information age and electronic devices. During this period the advancements, discoveries and inventions made by the Scientists include semiconductor transistors, development of the "theory and a process for growing monodisperse colloidal materials", technique of getting image of atoms arrangement on a sharp metals surface, integrated circuit and some other innovations.

The period of the 1940's to the 1960's, was the time of development in electronic field utilizing nanotechnology. The advances that were made during this time period proved to be crucial in the history of electronics. The experiments conducted took a lot of time and the success achieved was the result of continuous efforts of decades.

The integrated circuit was a milestone achievement by Jack Kilby in 1958 which made him eligible for winning the Noble Prize, although it was presented to him many years later (2000).

That was the time of invention, development and advancement in the study at atomic level which paved the way for Nanotechnology as we know it today.

The term Nanotechnology was coined by Professor Norio Taniguchi of Tokyo Science University in order to portray accuracy machining of materials to inside nuclear scale dimensional resiliencies.

Development in Nanotechnology is a step wise process during which many events took place at different times. The scientists were able to see the atom for the first time in 1981 when the "scanning tunnelling microscope" was invented. After this scientists worked harder and discover more valuable things. The 1980's was the time when the atom became the centre of many studies.

The Nanotech sector started to become more overtly commercial in 1990's when different companies started developing nanotechnology applications, patents and so forth.

Furthermore, more beneficial uses of this technology were identified after massive research efforts in both the public and private sectors. In 1993, "controlled synthesis of Nano-crystals" was developed which paved the path for Nanotech applications in the biological field.

At present nanotech is being used to develop 'DNA-like robotic nanoscale assembly devices'. It is also been used in the ongoing development of strategic plans regarding public health, safety and the environment.

Introducing Video

In order to have an effective video content strategy, the business will need to develop a roadmap outlining the coverage; the editorial direction; the aims; production; and the analytics of success.

In-short, some of the following questions should be addressed:

- ➔ Who is each video item aimed at?
- ➔ What are we hoping to accomplish?
- ➔ What topics will be covered?
- ➔ What do you want the viewer to take away from the video?
- ➔ How will the content be presented?
- ➔ What KPI's are you using to monitor performance?
- ➔ Who is responsible for creating the content; when; and how?
- ➔ Where will the content items sit on the portals?

Video Usage Statistics

In order to inform and guide video strategy, this section highlights some recent statistics that will better explain the changing face of the content business.

These statistics are worthy of your attention:

→ According to Cisco's Visual Networking Index, by the end of this year (2018), video-based traffic will account for 80 per cent of all consumer internet traffic
→ 59 percent of Executives would rather watch video than read text
→ 4x as many consumers would rather watch a video about a product then read about it
→ 74 per cent of millennials find video helpful
→ 60 per cent prefer to watch a video to reading a newsletter
→ 92 per cent of mobile video consumers share videos with others
→ Social video generates an astounding 1,200 per cent more shares than text and images combined
→ Publishers using video enjoy 41 per cent more web traffic from search than non-users
→ Video drives a whopping 157 per cent increase in organic traffic from Search Engines
→ Adding video to Emails increases the CTR by 200-300 per cent depending upon interest area
→ Combining video with full-page ads boosts engagement by 22 per cent
→ Property portal listings that include a video receive almost 400 per cent more inquiries than those without one
→ Fifty percent of executives look for more information after seeing a product or service in a video
→ 65 per cent of Executives visit the video marketer's website
→ 39 per cent call a vendor after viewing a video

➔ According to 70 per cent of marketers, video produces more conversions than any other type of content

➔ Including video on a landing page can increase conversion by 80 per cent

➔ The average conversion rate for websites using video is 4.9 per cent compared to 2.9 per cent for those that do not use video

➔ 74 per cent of users who watched an explainer video to learn more about a product or service ended up as purchasers

➔ 77 per cent of consumers say they've been convinced to buy a product or service by watching a video

➔ 90 per cent of users say that product videos are helpful in the decision making process

YouTube

YouTube offers the potential to generate both paid sign-ups AND a ton of ad sales revenue without paying commission.

The key things to remember with YouTube is the massive potential reach; and (importantly) the increased lifecycle of the content item. Video content of a review can last for years.

A timely 20 minute professional-looking review of Star Wars for example would likely yield >100k views over a 3-4 month period. This is far more than a text-based review would likely receive.

Facebook

Facebook's Mark Zuckerberg recently announced that the Facebook platform was generating in excess of 8 Billion video views per day.

It is therefore imperative that any and all free to access videos produced by the business are posted to Facebook.

Periscope

Periscope is a video streaming app owned and operated by Twitter. Due to its continued integration into the Twitter platform Periscope offers publishing businesses the opportunity to live stream on-the-fly using merely a mobile phone.

This method is suitable for lo-fi commentary, or live video rather than professional quality news-based editorial.

Other Video Websites

Lots of websites out there that the content producer can post to. I have listed my favourites, however other high traffic destinations include:

➔ VIMEO
➔ DAILY MOTION
➔ LIVELEAK
➔ META CAFÉ
➔ USTREAM

Studio Set-up

The following items are needed to successfully set up a studio to record video, podcasts and daily vlogs:

➔ HD video camera
➔ Sony Vegas Pro 14 editing suite

➜ Overlay graphics
➜ Intro files
➜ Outro files
➜ Chromakey background
➜ Basic lighting rig
➜ Snowball microphone

The total cost of this would be around AU$1,500, so in terms of initial outlay, quite affordable.

Performance

Once you have a studio set up as you wish you may want to experiment with content production techniques. One of the main issues will likely be how to best perform in front of the camera.

Some folk will like to prepare notes, a script even. Others however ill ad lib entirely.

The sample script included in the next section of this book could be inserted into either free, or premium teleprompter software.

The British manufacturer Autocue has a great software version of its teleprompter.

A Sample Script

OK, one of the projects I've been working on recently is a next-generation membership platform covering verticals within the emerging tech space... and as I have a webcam and studio set-up now I thought I would post my thoughts on the coming AI revolution... and how this subject will define the future of the more advanced economies in the world.

As some of you know, I have a keen interest in the business of AI. Indeed, certain product innovations I've looked at implementing with the platform involves aspects of AI, both in terms of the presentation of our proprietary structured data; ....through to voice-based machine learning, via the excellent Lyrebird API.

In terms of upcoming implications of AI, it's very much a rabbit hole. The more you information you garner about potential timelines; the more you realise that there is little agreement in business or academia. –For something so fundamental; and potentially species defining, I believe we need to better understand all the relevant risks and rewards.

Regarding risks, let's talk about a few.

I'll park the general fear that a logic-based machine will eventually decide that an often illogical humanity is the problem and find its own nefarious solution... as we are most likely a few decades away from that kind of implementation and threat.

However, we are reaching the period of time where we need to be asking ourselves whether it is in society's immediate interest to progress down this path with few, or no checks and balances.
Instead, I've concentrated on the potential disruption to one industry... the transportation sector... and how the one change symbiotically impacts an entire economy:

FIRST UP, JOBS – One of the most at risk professions in this early stage of the AI revolution will be drivers.

A quick scan of the internet outlines 3.5 million professional drivers, be they truck drivers, taxi drivers, Uber or bus drivers. By my reckoning this is some 4 per cent of all those active in the US labour force. If those jobs were to go over the next 5 years then you are looking at a deep economic recession, tax rises AND the resulting social unrest.

Indeed, a Forrester report from last year stated that some 6 per cent of all jobs would be lost due to AI by 2021... whilst an academic study from Oxford University stated that 47 per cent of all jobs are at risk from computerisation and/or automation.

This will lead to a massive changes in the economy; and likely increase the odds for Universal Basic Income... where all citizens are given a set amount of money per day, week, or month to live on.

This redistribution of wealth from the wealth creators within society to those who are no longer productive in the economy means a fundamental shift towards market socialism... a system that has never successfully been implemented.

Britain will be impacted massively too, with its 600,000 registered HGV drivers and some 300,000 taxi drivers. –Noting this, why did the British government give Millions of Pounds is R&D money to the automotive sector to advance automated driving?

Why did the US administration do the same?

What was the plan?

In terms of Australia, well... as it has some of the longest and most dangerous roads in the world; is one of the most urbanised countries in the world; and a high wage economy... my guess is that it too is primed for disruption in the transportation and logistics spaces.

SECONDLY, PERSONAL FREEDOM – Again, a wide ranging topic.

When automated cars become notably safer than human drivers... which is merely 1-2 years away, then how long will it be before humans are priced out of the marketplace by forever rising insurance premiums

FINALLY, HEALTHCARE – AI offers fantastic advances in pharma, biotech and healthcare.

However, it also has certain negative impacts. Problems that admittedly will eventually be solved by technology, but still impacts of note.

For example, if the number of car accidents is reduced to zero then the number of organ transplants able to take place will plummet.
I think I'm right in saying that there are more than 120,000 people already waiting for organ transplants in the US alone... and 16 per cent of all organ transplants are donated from victims of car accidents.

It's a dark subject to talk about, but certainly worth noting
I say again, I am very much for the advancement of machine learning and the myriad of opportunities it brings to human advancement.

I deem this advancement both necessary and inevitable. I just believe that a grown up discussion is needed on the implications for society both good and bad.

The question is, are our elected politicians and governments ready, willing, or able to discuss it in a non-partisan, mature way for the betterment of society?

Let's hope they are.

Anyway, I hope you've liked this video. If it gets sufficient traction, I may well post further riffs about AI, Augmented and Virtual Reality, Bioinformatics and all the other notable emerging technologies over the coming days and weeks.

This is just a bit of an experiment.

Take care... and thank you for your time!

The Content Wheel

This section of the document features a content wheel for typical membership websites.

It is always worth thinking about content types as and how they would appear in the proposition:

- ➜ Educate
- ➜ Inform
- ➜ Inspire
- ➜ Entertain
- ➜ Convince
- ➜ Support

Employee Stories

Behind the Scenes

How To's Guides

Industry Awards

R&A News

Bio's

Product Development

Media Mentions

Crowd Sourcing

Tales of Success

Industry Commentary

Press Releases

Predictions

Inspirational Stories

Good News

Breaking News

News

Timelines

Memes

Interviews

Podcasts

Blogs

Vlogs

Updates

Surveys

Diaries

Awards

Quiz

Photography

Polls

Screen Casts

Giveaways

Video

INSPIRE

INFORM

Live Chat

FAQ's

Illustrations

Sneak Peaks

Screenshots

Contests

ENTERTAIN

SUPPORT

Widgets

Customer Forums

Infographics

Competitions

Guides

Q&A's

Funny Stories

CONVINCE

EDUCATE

How To's

Tour

Parody Articles

Comics

Demo's

Ebooks

Music

Expert Interviews

Usage Guides

Free Trials

Reviews

Tutorials

Instructions

Ratings

User Stories

Awards

R&A

Poll Results

White Papers

Testimonials

Offers

Deals

How To's

Charts

Commentary

Endorsements

Coupon Codes

Research Papers

Tips

Lists

Walkthroughs

Price Guides

Analysis Reports

Studies

Mindmaps

Survey Results

Comparisons

Brochures

Quizzes

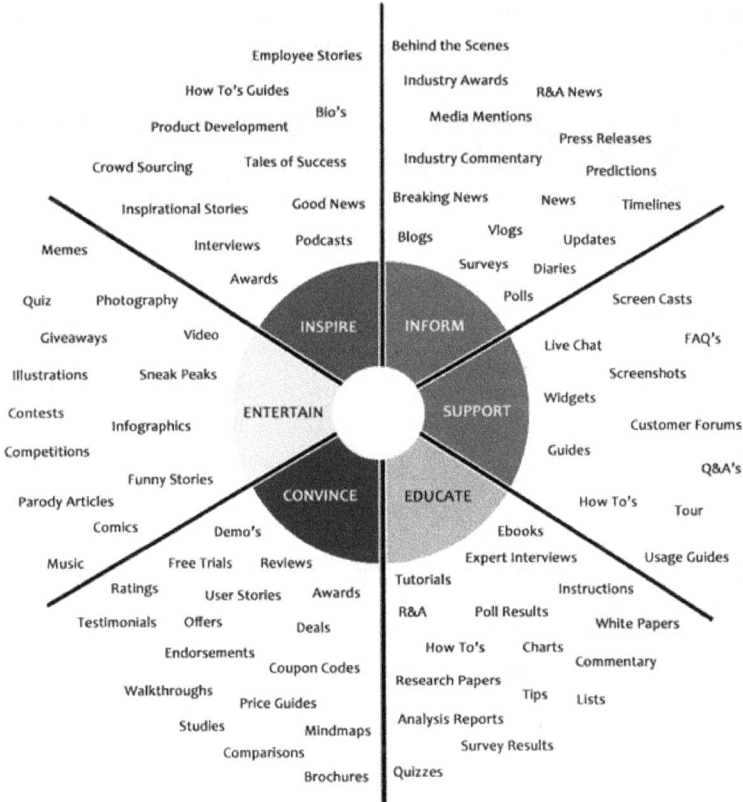

Content Value

Every single item of content produced and featured on the platform has two values associated to it. A value to the business and a value to the end user. More often than not, these values are one in the same.

This content value is displayed in the form of either a content ladder, or a more rudimentary diagram. For our example emerging technology platform business, we will display this in its simplest format with the most valuable content at the top, descending to the least valuable at the bottom.

The value and cost of production of these content items are also mirrored, with the cost of the most valuable content (e.g. R&A reports) being significantly higher than the cost of production for the cheapest content sets (e.g. rewritten corporate press releases).

Content Value Diagram

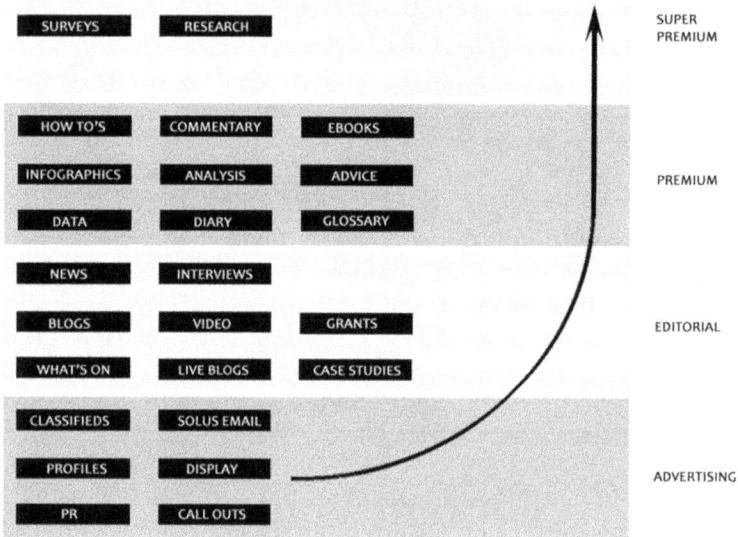

Content Production

The decision of what content to produce internally against what to outsource either overseas, or to contributors should be based around the proposition. I like the high quality content to be produced in-house as it is where I want the business IP and industry intelligence to sit.

In contrast, the content that should be outsourced would be rewritten product or company news, advertising-based content and listings. This is the 'grunt-work' for any portal.

In addition to the 'grunt work' outsourced content should include some advice-based columns and interviews with notable academics and/or CEO's within the emerging tech sectors.

For example, recruiters should be sought to offer advice to our members on how to advance their careers.

Finally, in the initial stages of creating this business it will be worthwhile outsourcing the writing of R&A reports to a specialist based in a lower wage economy such as the Philippines, or India. Both of these nations have exceptional skill and experience in writing formal documents based on proprietary data. Indeed, I have commissioned analysis of research data in both countries, with great success.

Internal Content

As part of this content strategy, the content produced internally includes the following:

➔ Industry news

→ Blogs
→ Commentary
→ Surveys
→ Data sets
→ Metrics
→ Evergreen content
→ Video
→ Diary
→ How To's
→ Guides
→ Glossary
→ SWOT reports
→ Industry profiles

External Content

Content produced externally either by outsourcing, or via the editorial contributor model will include the following:

→ Product news
→ Company news
→ Industry news
→ Job listings
→ Career advice
→ Commentary
→ PR
→ Classifieds
→ Case studies
→ Advice
→ What's on
→ Education
→ Events coverage
→ Company profiles, excluding SWOT's

→ Storefront profiles
→ Advertorial
→ R&A Reports

Contributor Payment Model

This section of the book outlines a new contributor model for the business.

Some analysis of the costs will be needed so as to ensure that it works economically.

The numbers provided are from memory based on what journalists would deem acceptable at the time (without organising protests... which lest we forget was threatened), through to a bonus based on the additional value the business received... under the assumption that some articles did very well, but most had little or no traction.

THE PROBLEM WITH THE CURRENT EDITORIAL MODEL

The quiescent yet reliable content model that has existed across the publishing sector for the best part of 450 years is no longer sustainable, with the most significant fissures being brought about by the ongoing digital revolution.

This paradigm shift has been caused by a change in the once reliable supply-demand ratio, with a huge oversupply of content in mass-market interest areas, or popular niches such as consumer technology, entertainment and culture; and nowhere near enough advertising Dollars willing or able to pay for it.

Under normal circumstances, long-established industries evolve through gradualism. The publishing sector however is in the midst of a vicennial upheaval. A sometimes velvet, but also sometimes messy revolution.

The results of which were first felt in newspapers, encyclopaedia's and other print publications, many of whom without a competitive business model floundered when confronted by the rise of free-to-access information websites and blogs in the late 1990's.

More recently however the change in the dynamics of the content business has impacted across all environments, including the previously usurping blogosphere.

Citizen journalists, along with vox populi bloggers, social media denizens, content spinners and marketing professionals have joined pro journalists; the establishment media commentariat; and industry/issue experts to create vast volumes of content matching their individual interest areas and life passions.

Whist this has fed the long-tail of organic search, it has also had an overwhelming effect on the competitive landscape for the most popular subject areas. The trend has in-turn spawned the rise of onshore and offshore content farms where article rewriting, including auto-magical content spinning purely to sell AdSense ads on keyword-rich, search engine optimised pages has become a prevalent and extremely profitable pox on the internet.

Google identified the problem long ago and has changed its algorithm multiple times to penalise what it defines as low quality content. The problem however has not gone away and 'content clutter' is still increasing.

When writing this essay, a simple search of Google News exemplified this best of all. Using the keyword "Obama", filtering for the past 24 hours returns nearly 71,000 results in the English language. A separate search for the Aussie rock band "AC/DC" yields some 15,000 articles over the same period.

Perhaps worryingly, the celebrity "Kim Kardashian" managed to be mentioned in nearly 3.3 million individual content mentions posted online over the past month. That may be a slow month by her 'break the internet' standards, but it is still a staggering 10,545 per cent more content items than the President of the world's second largest economy managed over the same period. Think about that for a moment.

Moving-forward, in order to succeed publishers and writers will need to adapt their strategies to better deal with a world where almost 90 per cent of native English speakers have access to the World Wide Web; with a further 400 million people from low wage economies such as India, Bangladesh and the Philippines having an increasingly good grasp of written English.

Together, the industry has to find a contributor payment model that is both fair and transparent to the external contributor; yet offers an acceptable return on investment to the publishing business.

THE NEED TO DIVERSIFY REVENUES IS ONLY INCREASING

As the acclaimed novelist Bill Bryson once said,

> *"In order to have quality journalism you need to have a good income stream and no internet model has produced a way of generating income that would pay for good-quality investigative journalism."*

Historically, Bryson is correct. However, profit through quality journalism is achievable even in a broad interest area such as politics, sport and the arts. Businesses simply need to be targeted; be focussed; add enough value; and be able to monetise content effectively.

This means (1) immersing themselves in the space they wish to occupy; (2) positioning themselves as the authority in the space; (3) garner usage; and (4) sell effectively.

A digital publisher will be successful if they do these things effectively.

Looking at the business of content from the publishers' perspective. Diversifying revenue streams is one of the key factors in the long-term success or failure of a venture once all capital raising opportunities have been exhausted.

Having worked through boom and bust cycles in the UK, US and Australian digital economies over the past 15-20 years I quickly learnt that diversifying revenue away from purely display advertising is vital to the long-term health of a publisher. The companies that are able to diversify successfully, whilst remembering to keep things simple will increase their odds of success.

"Keep it simple, execute well" is one of the most important mantra's to remember... and indeed used a number of times throughout this book.

Diversifying revenues away from purely advertising could mean anything from audience-based individual memberships; marketing-based corporate subscriptions; holding a regular networking event, or conference.

Alternatively, in attractive B2B verticals it could mean R&A activities, expert panels, or data-based sales.

By doing this, publishers will also be able to better invest in their lifeblood and primary IP, content.

BETTER VISUALIZATION AND IMMERSIVE CONTENT

The conflation of content innovation; contextualisation via new technologies; and audience development is something I have always believed in.

In the past, this has led me to building everything from conversation engines and prediction markets, through to sentiment analysis and performance algorithms designed with the aim of maximising usage, creating high-value content, or extending the lifecycle of the content item.

Today, the very same thoughts have me exploring the concepts behind immersive content and developing data visualisations.

In many way, immersive content is simply a continuing development in the art of storytelling. Interactivity within and/or around the content item; usage rewards and gamification features are coming to prominence.

The growing maturity of new technologies, especially HTML5, CSS3 and jQuery have enabled developers to create specific front-end functionalities and tools for storytelling across all devices. The huge ongoing increase in mobile usage has further driven standards and innovation across the digital economy.

Widely used SaaS tools such as Disqus' commenting service, or CoverItLive's 'live blogging' service are great and add to the users' experience on a property. Unique, proprietary functionality built solely with your property and its users in mind are even better. Editorial, however remains centre stage. Content is still king.

Driven by factors such as ever-increasing data transfer and processing power, the future of storytelling on the internet is undoubtedly going to be more visual and immersive in nature.

Professional writers should therefore look to embrace data visualisation, the art of illustration and interactive infographics in the same way they embraced taxonomies, search and user comments in the decade before.

When used in combination with well researched editorial the content item becomes an excellent tool for communication, engagement and ideally suited to the myriad of (viral) social media platforms out there. What's more, content farms and spinners are unlikely to compete at this level of communication.

Communities such as Facebook, Twitter and LinkedIn along with the larger social bookmarking properties like StumbleUpon and Reddit are key traffic drivers.

Today, Facebook and Twitter can each generate substantially more audience than organic search. That huge change has happened in just the last five years; and with that change, media properties like Buzzfeed have emerged and grown enormous audiences and bubble-like valuations of >$850 million by innovating with platforms and playing off viral social media content.

Whilst I doubt we have experienced peak Buzzfeed yet, will it still be amongst the very top content players in 5-10 years' time?

It might happen, but as its audience and therefore its advertising revenue are hugely reliant upon one entirely separate and unrelated business (Facebook) I would suggest that the odds are against it.

If I was to gaze into my figurative crystal ball and attempt to prognosticate the future, I would predict new brands based on the effective visualisation and communication of content emerging. They will experience a boom in traffic in the same way as Buzzfeed, the listicle, LOL cat meme's and pre-Panda content farms experienced before them.

EXAMPLES OF COMING CHANGE

Perhaps the coming 5G revolution will remove most (if not all) latency within Virtual Reality (VR) and Augmented Reality (AR) systems and therefore become a key driver in the next phase of innovation across the digital media ecosystem?

Conferences and learning could become truly virtual. Broadcast media could become deeply immersive and reporters could bring you the story, or sports, or whatever not just into your living room on an LCD screen, but further into your senses in near real-time.

Practically-speaking, you could immediately take a stroll around a house you are interested in buying, rather than waiting a few days for an open day.

Alternatively, you could go to a department store, scan curtains, or tiles and then transmogrify and/or renovate your own house and see detail as you would want to see it before you spend your money. The list of uses and potential innovation is almost endless.

Change is only 4-6 years away depending upon where you are located in the world, so now is the time for entrepreneurs within the media space to start imagining all those exciting new products and related business models.

DRIVING THE CONVERSATION FORWARD

Most editorial, particularly news-driven content, commentary and analysis is a conversation between the author and audience. The publisher could best be described as the conduit that enables the conversation to take place.

If you peer through the clouds of insipid Facebook status updates, utterly banal tweets and the narcissistic rage of the Instagram 'selfie', then you begin to see peoples maxims displayed for all to see. To attain traffic, gravitas and influence the writer needs to immerse themselves into the conversation on those platforms and exploit the social graph.

Successful journalism today requires that writers become much more than simply an investigator and wordsmith. The modern content producer needs to become the director of the conversation they have initiated through their storytelling; and partake in audience development activities revolving around the content items they have produced. In my experience, the better writers already do this.

Success ratios for writing demand that the content engages the reader. If the writer suffers from flaccidity in this critical area then they will need to have significant other weapons in their arsenal that can compensate to increase the profitability and therefore viability of their product.

INVESTIGATING THE INDUSTRY AVERAGE NUMBERS

For freelance contributors, it is worth taking the time to investigate the numbers that will more often than not dictate their potential career earnings.

For example, if a mid-sized, established website selling inventory using the CPM sales methodology has an average of three ad slots per page it will be likely be able to sell only one of these ad slots as premium (above the fold), with the other two positions being classed as non-premium and therefore less valuable.

According to research from Zenith, the median average premium display unit achieves a CPM (cost per mille) yield of $10.40, whilst the other ad units achieve about $1.90. Average the ad positions out and you have a CPM of $4.73.

Combined, the gross CPM of the page is $14.20, or about $0.01 per each page view. Now we have the gross number, let's use the amount of this available advertising inventory we would expect sold.

A sales team needs to be selling 70 per cent of its inventory in-house, hopefully all of it. Now let's use the average commission paid to the sales team of 12 per cent of gross. In order to break-even on an article that cost a paltry $100 to produce the publisher would need to serve nearly 11,500 page views over the content items usable life-cycle, which in the business of news is perhaps a mere 72 hours.

Caveat: the figures mentioned obviously change depending upon the subject matter, or vertical operating in; with the kind of content produced with B2B verticals securing significantly higher CPM's than mass-market content. Also, the numbers quoted are based on US averages across the entirety of the digital landscape, so not quite the same as the local numbers as say in Australia, or the UK.

Taking into account that the costs included in this calculation exclude absolutely all back office, sales and management support; the commissioning of the content item; the content items sub-editing should it be needed; and the loading of both the article and display ad's to their relevant platforms, you start to see a troubling story emerge.

If, upon doing these sums a contributor realises that the maximum publishers in their niche can pay them is $XYZ per article then that writer can then make an informed judgement call as to whether the subject area they are currently writing in is viable for them.

If writers decide the monetary value of the content in the marketplace means they cannot make enough money from it then they could look to move into areas where the over-supply of content either does not exist, or is significantly less pronounced.

The market decides the price of content.

A NEW TAKE ON CONTRIBUTOR PAYMENT MODELS

First and foremost most publishers have an in-house team of journalists and content producers. In addition to the in-house team, most publishers use external contributors to garner enhanced commentary on specialist subjects or unique riff's. Good publishers appreciate and value the content that each member of this extended editorial family brings to the business.

Additionally, a good publisher should always desire external writers and influencers to know that if they have news to break, or something of significance to say in their horizontal/vertical/interest area then they will make more money by posting that story on their platform rather than at their competitor(s).

In order to be fair to the contributor, a publisher should ignore the trend of not paying for their labour, as rumoured at HuffPo and countless others both here in Australia and across the rest of the globalised world.

Pro-active publishers should also ignore the low rates seen on most legacy print publications digital channels. Lots of publications pay their external contributors peanuts (c$10-25 per article) for well researched 500-1,000 word articles, using the inherent passion of the contributor against them. In high wage economies I deem this unfair; more than a little cynical; and certainly a key factor in the erosion of the differentiation between professional journalism; and the hobbyist.

Additionally, publishers should never lose fight of the fact that they are in a symbiotic relationship with their content suppliers. In the long-run, the rush to the bottom will prove entirely self-defeating for most properties and for the industry as a whole.

Instead, it is my view that publishers should investigate a scalable contributor payment model based around a sound libertarian principal that's very close to my heart, the *meritocracy*. With this new meritocratic model publishers will be able to pay external contributors both for their time, via a flat fee for production time; and then a progressive (banded) payment based on the amount of people that view the content during its typical one-month lifespan. No multiple payments, or needless complexity. Just a payment for time and one payment one month later for performance.

Using this model, if an external contributors article garners few views and little value for the business then the writer will earn only a small payment; as befitting journalism that is worth less to the business. The cream should always be allowed to rise to the top.

TRANSPARENCY IS NOT OPTIONAL

A simple question - does the average contributor know how much traffic their latest article generated?

More often than not, they will never be informed instead, it will be left to somebody in the editorial team to judge quality. I believe this is a fundamental strategic error.

In terms of transparency, I believe every paid contributor to a publisher should know how many unique browsers their individual article has generated over the 30 day agreed lifecycle. This helps the writer better understand what works and doesn't work on the property... and therefore improve both for the betterment of their own career and the business they are working for.

It is true that over the past 4-5 years a few notable mass-market publications in the UK and US marketplaces have experimented with 'progressive' payment models somewhat similar to the proposal explained here.

They have however missed one key attribute, the actual time required by the writer to produce the article.

The old model meant that the writer will likely only get paid for the article if it is read by a predetermined (and inevitably huge) number of eye balls, which means that for the majority of the time they are writing for the publisher for free. To make matters worse the contributor does not even know the number of visitors their article generated. Again, this equates to the same long-term result of driving down quality.

High quality editorial is a serious endeavour and the better publishers out there should have the intention not just to back it in theory, but to become the standard by which others are judged.

When folk suggest that utilising a new payment model risks losing existing contributor relationships because it is based on merit, I do not understand the logic. In my eyes, it assumes the person does not value what they are writing; and if they as the producer do not value their product then why produce that product in the first place and/or expect others to value it?

Of course I expect some within the profession would dislike the proposed system, as it means change. Many within publishing are terrified of change; still want to be paid by the word, which lest we forget is an entirely unsustainable way of operating in the digital environment; and are guilty of assuming the worst without first gaining a comprehensive understanding of the causation.

Will a new meritocratic payment system work for all publishers?

No, but I do firmly believe the future for online-only editorial exists in concepts such as this. For the reasons I have outlined in this article, I do not believe the existing models have sustainable long-term futures.

Evolutionary economics tells us that in order to prosper we must evolve and adapt. The publishing sector is not exempt from this. It is now time for both journalist and publisher to adapt.

THE MODEL

The table below outlines the model, complete with the bands we are starting with. It is our expectation that with all the Contributor-produced content being within the guidelines of a Metered Paywall (meaning everybody can initially access the content) then the average page view per article produced would be somewhere north of 2,000.

We have however seen some recent articles garner more than ten-times that amount.

Minimum unique views	Base rate	Bonus paid	Payment per article
0-249	$115	$0	$115
250-499	$115	$10	$125
500-749	$115	$15	$130
750-999	$115	$20	$135
1,000-1,999	$115	$25	$140
2,000-4,999	$115	$45	$160
5,000-9,999	$115	$85	$200
10,000-12,499	$115	$145	$260
12,50-14,999	$115	$225	$340
15,000-17,499	$115	$325	$440
17,500-19,999	$115	$445	$560
20,000+	$115	$585	$700

In addition to the financial aspects of this model, all our contributors will be given a complimentary (monthly) subscription to the platform. They'll receive free access to the reputation management toolkit, the industry glossary, education-listings, career-related content and job search will be of continuous value to the writer's career.

So, in order to summarise, the business would be (1) paying contributors for the creation of the article; (2) offering a transparent and attractive bonus system for writers; and (3) supplying complimentary access to premium tools, content and services.

That is a good deal and reinforces our commitment to quality journalism and the industry as a whole.

Editorial Calendar and Diary

An editorial calendar outlining publishing dates, results, special events and occasions, et cetera should be created in order to ensure that no major event is missed. Pre-planning of time and resource is essential for an effective and efficient content plan.

Language and Editorial Style

For any publishing business with a number of contributors it is vital to have a style guide. This ensures that the content producers are using the same grammar and spellings across the site (and potentially across the world).

Implementation

The Editor, Content Director, or Editor in Chief of the website, or publication should produce a Style Guide for use on the property. This should be referenced so that all contributors can follow it.

The Banned List

Within the community section, certain profanities will be filtered out. Rather than list a huge number of slang words and swear words and thus weird you all out, I'll leave you to use your imagination as to what words to filter.

If you cannot think of any (!?!?) then it would be a good move to download a list of words from the internet, or utilise a prebuilt profanity filter. A number of organisations exist in this space, including Web Purify, PurgoMalum and PubNub.

Be Viral

Having a Metered Paywall is key to this as it would allow the business to push an individual article and then potentially link through to other related articles within the article itself. Those that are passionate about the subject will then subscribe as they have potentially used all the available articles a free subscription allows them to do over a set period.

In terms of the content, quite often the success or failure of an article is based solely upon its headline.

Based on this, it would be wise to ensure that the editorial team (and contributors) spend time and/or sub-edit each article produced to ensure that it is as *vital* to the potential user as possible. Each new article should be written with the thought that it costs X to produce and as a result the business needs to see Y in terms of resulting value to the business.

Getting killer quotes and then spending a few minutes to genuinely push the article on social media (above and beyond simply posting it) then the writer can generate a buzz and encourage usage. By getting the headline and key quotes within the riff the editor increases the attractiveness both of the article and the overall subscription.

Editorial KPI's

In this section of the book I am exploring the metrics that can be used to measure the effectiveness of the content on any platform.

For online publications, the Editor in Chief should be monitoring all the below metrics by portal and buy content producer. They should be compiling these with the help of the audience development professional.

The data is sourced from the Email broadcasting software, from the web analytics software you are using (e.g. Google Analytics) and from your own internal metrics.

Whilst this might seem like an onerous task, when compiled on a monthly basis, the Board, yourself and your management team will be able to garner a far better understanding of what is and is not working on the platform.

It goes without saying that this is absolutely vital to the health and scalability of the business.

Top-level Metrics

→ Total unique browsers
→ Total visits
→ Total page impressions
→ Percentage of traffic by content type
→ Total conversions
→ Bounce rate
→ Average time of content item
→ Average time on site
→ Average cost per content item
→ Average value to be business per content item
→ Top 20 content items
→ Total social media reach
→ Renewal rate (by site)
→ Traffic breakdown (by referral type)
→ Traffic breakdown (by geography)
→ Traffic breakdown (by device/medium)
→ Traffic breakdown (by operating system)
→ Total membership
→ Membership growth rate (by month)

Production Metrics

→ Total content items produced
→ Content items (by staff member)
→ Content items (by contributor)
→ Content items (by content type)
→ Content items (by taxonomy/site)

- ➔ Average words per article (by author)
- ➔ Average words per article (by team)
- ➔ Average words per article (by content type)
- ➔ Average words per article (by taxonomy/site)
- ➔ Monthly content items (by staff member)
- ➔ Monthly content items (by contributor)
- ➔ Monthly content items (by content type)
- ➔ Monthly content items (by taxonomy/site)
- ➔ Average cost per content item (by staff member)
- ➔ Average cost per article (by contributor)
- ➔ Average cost per article (by content type)
- ➔ Average cost per article (by taxonomy/site)
- ➔ Total cost of production
- ➔ Total cost of production (percentage breakdown)
- ➔ Average value to the business (by staff member)
- ➔ Average value to the business (by contributor)
- ➔ Average value to the business (by content type)
- ➔ Average value to the business (by taxonomy/site)

Social Media Metrics

- ➔ Twitter followers (by account/site)
- ➔ Twitter followers (monthly growth)
- ➔ Twitter likes (by account/site)
- ➔ Twitter likes (by staff member)
- ➔ Twitter likes (by contributor)
- ➔ Top performing Twitter likes
- ➔ Twitter likes (monthly growth)
- ➔ Twitter retweets (by account/site)
- ➔ Twitter retweets (by staff member)
- ➔ Twitter retweets (by contributor)
- ➔ Top performing Twitter retweets
- ➔ Average daily posts (by account)

→ Total unique browsers from Twitter
→ Total visits by from Twitter
→ Total page impressions from Twitter
→ Conversions generated by Twitter (by account/site)
→ Total reach from Twitter (by account/site)
→ Follower growth from Twitter
→ ROI for Twitter campaigns (organic)
→ ROI for Twitter campaigns (paid)
→ Average cost per subscriber from Twitter (organic)
→ Average cost per subscriber from Twitter (paid)
→ Facebook followers (by account/site)
→ Facebook followers (monthly growth)
→ Facebook likes (by account/site)
→ Facebook likes (by staff member)
→ Facebook likes (by contributor)
→ Top performing Facebook likes
→ Facebook likes (monthly growth)
→ Facebook mentions (by account/site)
→ Facebook mentions (by staff member)
→ Facebook mentions (by contributor)
→ Top performing Facebook mentions
→ Average daily posts (by account)
→ Total unique browsers from Facebook
→ Total visits by from Facebook
→ Total page impressions from Facebook
→ Follower growth on Facebook
→ Conversions generated by Facebook (by account/site)
→ Total reach from Facebook (by account/site)
→ ROI for Facebook campaigns (organic)
→ ROI for Facebook campaigns (paid)
→ Average cost per subscriber from Facebook (organic)
→ Average cost per subscriber from Facebook (paid)
→ Instagram followers (by account/site)
→ Instagram followers (monthly growth)
→ Instagram likes (by account/site)

- ➔ Instagram likes (by staff member)
- ➔ Instagram likes (by contributor)
- ➔ Top performing Instagram likes
- ➔ Instagram likes (monthly growth)
- ➔ Instagram follower growth
- ➔ Average daily posts (by account)
- ➔ Total unique browsers from Instagram
- ➔ Total visits by from Instagram
- ➔ Total page impressions from Instagram
- ➔ Conversions generated by Instagram (by account/site)
- ➔ Total reach from Instagram (by account/site)
- ➔ ROI for Instagram campaigns (organic)
- ➔ ROI for Instagram campaigns (paid)
- ➔ Average cost per subscriber from Instagram (organic)
- ➔ Average cost per subscriber from Instagram (paid)
- ➔ LinkedIn follower growth
- ➔ LinkedIn followers (Company page)
- ➔ LinkedIn followers (Company monthly growth)
- ➔ LinkedIn likes (by account/site)
- ➔ LinkedIn likes (by staff member)
- ➔ LinkedIn likes (by contributor)
- ➔ Top performing LinkedIn likes
- ➔ LinkedIn likes (monthly growth)
- ➔ Average daily posts
- ➔ LinkedIn groups (by subscriber volume)
- ➔ Total unique browsers from LinkedIn
- ➔ Total visits by from LinkedIn
- ➔ Total page impressions from LinkedIn
- ➔ Conversions generated by LinkedIn (by account/site)
- ➔ Total reach from LinkedIn (by account/site)
- ➔ ROI for LinkedIn campaigns (organic)
- ➔ ROI for LinkedIn campaigns (paid)
- ➔ Average cost per subscriber from LinkedIn (organic)
- ➔ Average cost per subscriber from LinkedIn (paid)
- ➔ Other social media growth (unique browsers)

→ Other social media growth (by visits)
→ Other social media growth (by page impressions0
→ Other social media growth (by reach)
→ Other social media growth (by content type)
→ Other social media growth (by account/site)
→ Other social media growth (by link)
→ ROI from other social media growth

Conversion Metrics

→ Total monthly goal conversions
→ Goal conversion rate
→ Average time to purchase
→ Funnel analysis (by source)
→ Funnel analysis (by content type)
→ Funnel analysis (trend)
→ Upsale generated (number)
→ Number of transactions (by content type)
→ Number of transactions (by taxonomy/site)
→ Number of transactions (by source)
→ Cost per transaction (by source)
→ Cost per transaction (by taxonomy/site)
→ Cost per transaction (by landing page)
→ Cost per transaction (by content type)
→ Average time to conversion
→ Customer acquisition cost (breakdown)

Email / Newsletter Metrics

→ Subscriber universe
→ List sizes
→ Average open rate

- ➜ Open rate (by broadcast)
- ➜ Open rate (by date)
- ➜ Open rate (by format)
- ➜ Average CTR
- ➜ Average CTR (by format)
- ➜ Average CTR (by broadcast)
- ➜ Best performing subject lines
- ➜ Best performing subject lines (by broadcast)
- ➜ Best performing subject lines (by list)
- ➜ Visits generated (by link)
- ➜ Visits generated (by content type)
- ➜ Visits generated (by format)
- ➜ Visits generated (by date)
- ➜ Visits generated (by broadcast)
- ➜ Page views per visit (by content item)
- ➜ Page views per visit (by broadcast)
- ➜ Page views per visit (by link)
- ➜ Average page views per visit
- ➜ Average bounce rate
- ➜ Bounce rate (by broadcast)
- ➜ Bounce rate (by list)
- ➜ Average unsubscribe rate (by list)
- ➜ Average unsubscribe rate (by date)
- ➜ Average unsubscribe rate (by broadcast)
- ➜ Number of SPAM complaints*

* No matter what you do, you will always receive a limited number of spam complaints from recipients and ex-members.

Engagement Metrics

- ➜ Average time on content item (by staff member)
- ➜ Average time on content item (by contributor)

→ Average time on content item (by content type)
→ Average time on content item (by taxonomy/site)
→ New versus returning
→ Average time on site
→ Average bounce rate (by content type)
→ Average bounce rate (by staff member)
→ Average bounce rate (by contributor)
→ Average bounce rate (by taxonomy/site)
→ Average bounce rate (by source)
→ Twitter comments (by content type)
→ Twitter comments (by staff member)
→ Twitter comments (by contributor)
→ Twitter comments (by taxonomy/site)
→ Top Twitter comments (by volume)
→ Facebook comments (by content type)
→ Facebook comments (by staff member)
→ Facebook comments (by contributor)
→ Facebook comments (by taxonomy/site)
→ Top Facebook comments (by volume)
→ Instagram comments (by content item)
→ Instagram comments (by staff member)
→ Instagram comments (by contributor)
→ Top Instagram comments (by volume)
→ LinkedIn comments (by content type)
→ LinkedIn comments (by taxonomy/site)
→ LinkedIn comments (by staff member)
→ LinkedIn comments (by contributor)
→ Top LinkedIn comments (by volume)
→ Page views per session (by taxonomy/site)
→ Page views per session (by staff member)
→ Page views per session (by contributor)
→ Page views per session (by source)
→ Page views per session (by content type)
→ Page views per session (trend)

CHAPTER 8

Building a Directory

E ach portal will have a directory consisting of the industry profiles mentioned earlier in this book. The aim would be to launch each property with 50-100 company profiles each.

The Concept

The portals would include the database of company profiles and list them in a unique company index. Doing this, rather than arranging merely by taxonomy, or by alphabet immediately increases the perception of value to the end user.

For example, within the nanotechnology sector it would be called the 'NanoTech 100', or if you wanted to include the portals branding then you would simply add the branding to the beginning of the name. For example, the XYZ NanoTech 100 Index.

The index is an ambitious, next-generation directory of organisations working within the stipulated niche. Each news release and associated corporate is scored; the company benchmarked; and then its performance ranked using a proprietary algorithm.

Scoring Mechanisms

The scoring mechanism for each company listed in the index consists of the following attributes:

SOCIAL SENTIMENT

This consists of four separate scores ranging from 0 to 100, which are contributed by members of the community. The first score is based on 'Brand Strength'; the second on 'Business Innovation'; the third on 'Management Strength'; and the fourth on 'Overall Business Performance'.

IPs' and membership details are logged for each score to ensure the purity of the model. This is important to the

COMPUTATIONAL

This attribute relates to how popular the item is within the platform. More credibility and gravitas is given to the articles that have garnered more attention within the system. This essentially acts as a magnifying glass.

ANALYSIS-BASED

This attribute consists of an in-house human analyst scoring the company based on its financial results; product pipeline; or other notable statement released. The exact same scoring methodology as used in the social sentiment scoring mechanism is used, only this time from within the CMS by the editorial team.

Within the algorithm, additional weight is carried from the analysis-based score over and above the other scoring attributes. Again, this protects the purity of the model against potential manipulations.

Benchmarking and Ranking

Once a score is allocated to each news item relating to a specific company then the company receives that score. The score that has been allocated then allows the company mentioned to be ranked against its peers and competitors. From this ranking a benchmark score can be garnered.

The key advantages of this model are (1) after a few months of scoring proprietary research data is generated for the niche; (2) it motivates usage on a corporate level; and (3) it centres the industry concerned on the portal, thus making the business more necessary and vital to the end user.

CHAPTER 9

Marketing Strategy

So far in this book we have looked at the strategy, the platform and the product specification. Now, it is time to look in more detail at the marketing strategy.

In the section immediately following this I will concentrate on audience development tactics and maximising usage. For now though we will concentrate on marketing.

Marketing strategy is an ongoing, forward-looking approach to planning, with the defined goal of achieving a sustainable competitive advantage over any/all potential competitors.

It is absolutely vital that any business develops a strong, well thought out marketing strategy. Without one, the efforts to breakthrough and attract customers at a scalable ROI are likely to fail.

In terms of our example business, the strategy should be making sure that both the subscription-based products and the single copy reports meet customer requirements and therefore enable the business to develop a long-term and profitable relationships with professionals working within the target sectors.

To best achieve this, the marketing team will need to create a superior and agile and flexible strategy that can respond to changes to the industry, the landscape and awareness of the product.

The purpose of the strategy should be to identify and then communicate the key benefits of your business offering to your target market. The strategy needs to be about attracting and informing potential customers.

Once implemented, it is imperative that the business monitors the success of the marketing strategy. It can do this by setting suitable KPI's. These will be explained in considerable detail in a later section of this book.

The 7 P's of Marketing

The 7 P's marketing model was originally devised by E Jerome McCarthy in his 1960 book 'Basic Marketing. A Managerial Approach'.
In my personal opinion, it is still worth keeping the '7 P's of marketing' in mind as you develop a marketing strategy.

PRODUCT – This refers to what the business is selling. Success is often defined by including, defining and prioritising the features, functionalities; the main reasons to purchase the product; and highlights what problem, or problems the product solves.

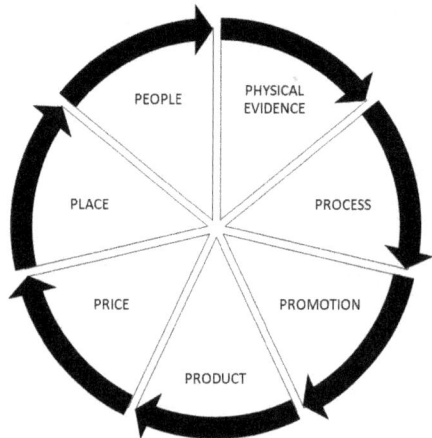

The business can utilise research and development activities, or analysis in order to gauge potential new products, or product developments.

PROMOTION – This refers to the promotional activities and marketing tactics the business will use to make potential customers aware of the available products.

It includes most audience development activities such as PPC advertising, but also involves the fundamental sales tactics along with any/all promotions.

PRICE – This 'P' refers to the pricing strategy and resulting pricing structure for the products and how this will affect customers.

Any business should identify how much customers are prepared to pay for the product; how much margin is required; the payments methods; payment terms; any promotional offers; and any other costs.

PLACE – This simply refers to where your products are created, sold, or distributed.

The example business is online only, but worth remembering that many media businesses have physical businesses alongside them, such as networking events and/or magazines sold in retail outlets.

PEOPLE – This refers to the team and contributors that work for your business. When the business provides good customer service to members it will create a positive experience. This has the potential to lead to new opportunity.

PROCESS – This 'P' refers to the processes and procedures involved in delivering the subscriptions and single-copy products to the customer. Having efficient processes in place ensures that the business both delivers the same standard of service to your customers time and time again; and increases its overall efficiency.

PHYSICAL EVIDENCE – From the look and feel of the portals to the branding of the business, this refers to everything customers see when interacting with the business.

Better Understanding the Audience

As with all membership, or circulation-based businesses our example portal business will need to understand its audience as much as it can. Some of this understanding can be sourced from survey data and focus groups, but other information can be extracted from the membership database itself.

For example, in terms of how long the users have subscribed, what is the actual breakdown?

By understanding this data the business owner can better respond, tailor the product and prognosticate the results from any and all marketing activities.

Surveys

Before you go to the time/energy and potentially cost of performing a survey of professionals within your industry you should ask yourself a few questions, such as:

- ➜ What is the desired end result?
- ➜ Who is your target audience?
- ➜ Is a telephone, qualitative (focus group), or online survey preferable?
- ➜ How will I motivate people to participate?
- ➜ Are my questions specific, yet neutral enough?

➔ How will I utilise the information collected?

➔ Can the content be reused?

Each individual business in each individual sector will have its own distinct questions and requirements, but typical survey questions to ask your audience will include (in no particular order):

➔ How long has your organisation been in business?

➔ In which industry is your organisation

➔ How many employees does your organisation have?

➔ Is your organisation within the public, or private sector?

➔ What is your industry outlook for the next 12 months?

➔ How long have you been in your present role?

➔ Are you looking to change roles in the next 12 months?

➔ What was the businesses annual turnover for your organisation in the last financial year?

➔ Who are your customers?

Member Personas

Understanding who your potential buyers (members) are is vital to conversion rates and marketing success. This books example business publishes portals aimed at professionals working within stipulated emerging technology verticals. The business needs to target these people, not people that work in administration, or back office at Retail Banks.

To better understand and target them it is worth noting as many facts about them as possible.

For example, age, location, job title, defined role, organisation size, education, values, financials, procurement privileges, decision maker, et cetera.

An example buyer persona for our emerging technology business would be:

Age: 21 - 65+
Job Title: Scientific Team Leader
Location: Sydney, Australia
Role: Scientific
Organisation Size: SMB
Education: Post Graduate
Income: $80-250,000
Values: Job search and accessing R&A data sets
Procurement rights: Yes, up to $10,000
Decision Maker: Yes

In other sectors, especially consumer the list will be far larger. They could include anything from age, gender, relationship status, shopping habits and so on.

I like to view buyer personas as working symbiotically with the product specification. This ensures that the product is always solving issues that matter to the prospective buyer.

When researching new products it is always wise to keep this in mind. Do a search on LinkedIn and look for how many professionals are listed on their using similar describers to your buyer personas. You can do this by filtering and searching using the facetted search they have on that platform. The answer should help dictate your views as to the potential size of your audience... and therefore the scalability of your business.

Competitive Intelligence and Benchmarking

Top-level competitive analysis for each and every portal should be carried out as part of the product development strategy. This activity should consist of both a SWOT analysis and also a functional and content benchmarking document.

Introducing Influencers

Influencer marketing is simply a portion of the marketing mix, which focuses effort on influential people rather than the target market as a whole. It identifies the individuals that have most influence over potential buyers and then orients marketing activities around these influencers. These influencers then use their reach and influence within the market to popularise products.

Engagement Pods

Engagement Pod is a private group of people with similar audiences ready to engage with each other's content on social media. This engagement boosts the relevance and reach of each person's content on most social media outlets, but certainly works on Instagram and LinkedIn.

Find an Angle

To be successful with influencer marketing a business needs to find an angle. A way of presenting its offering to influencers. Some thought and care needs to be taken to garner tangible success. –Remember, if successful, it could be business defining.

E-PR

The business is a publisher covering defined industry verticals. As a result the business needs to lay claim to those verticals and become monopolies within the space. Ubiquitous and necessary to all that want to participate in the sector.

To achieve this, one of the key requirements is for the business to be narcissistic in outlook. It needs to not only insert itself into the conversation, but also to drive the conversation.

One way of doing this is by launching the Contributor Payment Model. It will be noteworthy with some 'old school' journalists pontificating manically about how evil it is, but with others, especially on the publishing-side knowing and understanding the obvious benefits of the model. Make no mistake, this model is likely the best case scenario for journalists over the coming decades as the news model is entirely broken.

PR Production

One of the key tools in a business's arsenal is PR. The business should be utilising PR to the max as the potential to become newsworthy within the space is high.

In order to produce PR rather than hand this over to an editorial team, it will be worth giving this to a marketing person to write, and based on editorial feedback.

It is worth creating one PR release every fortnight.

PR Distribution

It is worth distributing each press release to as many potential sources as possible. You want it to be featured everywhere, not just in Australia, or the UK, or US. The guiding principal should be that if it is newsworthy, then it is newsworthy.

The business should therefore look to strike a deal with a PR distribution service which means that each release would cost about $200, tops.

Once the press release has been distributed most PR broadcasters such as PR NewsWire, or PRWire offer detailed analytics on various usage metrics.

Offline Marketing

It is always wise to look at all the options to market your business. These options undoubtedly include offline channels as well as online.

One of the significant types of offline marketing relevant to this business is speaking at conferences/events/workshops relevant to both the subject and the platform business, or on broadcast media, where the business will gain additional gravitas and brand awareness.

Additionally, it will be worth looking at potential unsold inventory swaps with business magazines in relevant spaces. These could be either subject-specific, or role-specific, depending upon the reason for advertising.

One of the more effective methods of marketing the business would be writing advertorials and/or issue-related articles centred on the business and its coverage.

Partnerships

Partnerships with conferences and events businesses is one way to insert the business into the industry.

The make-up of a partnership deal could be, one ticket to the conference, plus the attendee list in return for the business marketing the conference on the website and to its members; and the promise of coverage. This kind of deal is mutually beneficial and enables the business to position itself at the centre of the desired industry verticals.

CHAPTER 10

Audience Development

The definition of 'audience development' is fluid and (at present) not defined particularly well. However, within the scope of this book I define audience development as distinct activities undertaken specifically (1) drive traffic to the destination website; (2) to maximise usage of the destination website by the audience; and (3) to increase conversions and sales by measurement and optimisation.

General Tips for Traffic Growth

The general tips within this section of the book act as a top-level guide as to the tasks.

I will dig deeper into many of the points and relate them to other methodologies and tasks later in this chapter.

Research and Competitive Analysis

➜ Discover what your primary competitors are doing?
➜ Benchmark your property against the top 3-4 relevant competitors, or businesses in similar spaces
➜ Profile the potential audience and industry as a whole
➜ Discover what functionality and/or content the industry desires most

Everything Leads to Rome

Every single activity undertaken must generate revenue either directly via sales, or indirectly via usage or brand awareness. All efforts must lead to Rome

Prioritise

➜ Ensure that the business is producing the correct content mix and/or functionality to enable you to extract maximum usage and value from each user
➜ Produce evergreen content that has a long shelf-life. The quality of this content should be as high as possible
➜ Increase the Bang per Buck of the effort by ensuring that the business prioritises audience generating platforms over and above all others. Basically, do not waste time

Set Targets and Goals

➜ Identify key goals and objectives. What are you trying to achieve? Concentrate relentlessly on that and do not attempt to dilute the idea and/or concept to hit other supplementary but less important goals.

➔ Ensure you can measure your progress against targets honestly and objectively

➔ Be conservative in your reporting of actuals, especially in terms of the top-level stats

➔ Set goals and milestones that are achievable... and ramp. Always be growing

➔ Break tasks down into suitable chunks. Chunks that are achievable over a stipulated period of time. This is both realistic and motivating.

Social Media Activities

➔ Ensure that the business and (especially) the editorial team are immersed within the relevant industry groups, communities and networks. Remember that this means not simply promoting the business, but promoting the business and community surrounding it. Historically, I have used a four posts to one link to home content methodology on social bookmarking sites such as StumbleUpon, Digg and Reddit. I suspect the same strategy works today

➔ Target the correct demographics, industry verticals and special interest groups

➔ Be viral

SEO

➔ Run tests using popular Firefox and/or Firefox SEO-focussed toolbars and plugins, along with Google Analytics and Webmaster Tools

→ Make amendments to the portals based on the recommendations returned. Take special note of (1) speed; (2) crawlability; (3) text to code ratio; and (4) code errors

→ Benchmark the results against other properties in order to gauge how competitive the site is. Personally, I like to do this after every iteration

→ Seek out the highest quality links, including those with a .edu or .gov domain extensions

→ Ensure the source code is clean

→ Optimise the sales funnel

→ Constantly and relentlessly hone the marketing spend and mix in order to generate the best possible ROI from not just the budget, but also in terms of effort

→ Always seek new opportunity

Ensure Value

→ Test the product. Where you see specific weaknesses amend. Do this in an ongoing progressive way to ensure constant innovation and that the product meets an evolving industry

→ Get the potential audience talking about the product

→ Garner testimonials from members to reinforce the sales proposition

→ Create and distribute suitable surveys and polls to ensure the product meets the users requirements

→ Create training literature and/or walkthrough videos to maximise the usage of existing members

→ Commission and/or produce videos, white papers, eBooks and reports to reinforce the proposition and generate leads for the business

Establishing Authority

➜ Authority, credible, gravitas, trusted, expert and resource are important describing words any industry portal should strive for. Authority develops usage and trust. Credibility establishes the business as 'expert'. Resource equates to usefulness and relevance to professionals working within the sector.

➜ Always look for ways to build tangible recognition, citations in publications and mentions within related communities

➜ Try to create a buzz around both the business and the industry.

➜ Be passionate. Membership business seen by professionals working as being an advocate for the industry they operate within and are often passionate about equates to those professionals being passionate and loyal to the business.

Understanding the Propositions

One of the main factors in whether a business is successful or not is whether the staff actually understand the core propositions for the user through to the paying subscriber. If staff do not understand the product then how on earth are the end users meant to understand?

I could have included this section of the book elsewhere within the overall structure, but decided to include it here because the role of audience development at the business is to understand; and to explain; and motivate; and target the correct potential users to the correct product. The team performing audience development *have* to know the product inside out, upside down and backwards.

Presenting value

The website will need to immediately explain what it is. The URL, branding and user interface will help, but short and precise sentences will work wonders.

> XYZ is the industry-leading destination portal for professionals working within the global XYZ sector.
>
> Our content sets range from the latest company news, deals, products and profiles through to in-depth industry news, market profiles, expert analysis and hard-to-source research data.
>
> In addition to our company and industry-level coverage we offer professionals a global view of the jobs market within the sector with the definitive global jobs board for the sector.
>
> XYZ is dedicated to the XYZ industry.

Below is an outline of the value proposition for the subscription packages, complete with subscription options:

INDIVIDUAL SUBSCRIPTION

The individual subscription is the main product for the business and as a result it needs to have a proposition that is both effective immediately and also offers long term value.

The proposition has the following attributes and is described below in plain language:

➔ **JOBS**
- o View unlimited jobs
- o AI interface

➔ **NEWS**
- o Product news
- o Company news
- o Industry news
- o Industry diary
- o Industry commentary
- o R&A news
- o Video
- o Collated news
- o Blog
- o Newsletters

➔ **GUIDES**
- o How to's
- o Industry guides
- o Salary survey results
- o Standardised job descriptions
- o Career advice articles

➔ **EDUCATION**
- o Search education courses
- o Career paths

➔ **COMMUNITY**
- o Browse members
- o Search members

➔ **MARKETING**
- o SaaS social media posting
- o SaaS reputation management
- o Resources

➔ **R&A**
- o Access to proprietary data sets
- o Access the deals database
- o Access to company profiles (excluding SWOT's)

    o   Access to country-specific industry profiles
    o   Access to survey results
    o   Access to the industry glossary
    o   Ask the expert

The subscription options for this product are:

ANNUAL SUBSCRIPTION – With this subscription the individual pays upfront for the annual subscription at a reduced price. The subscription then auto-renews every year.

PAY MONTHLY ANNUAL SUBSCRIPTION – This subscription is for a 12 month period, but enables the individual member to pay on a monthly basis. This subscription has a higher yield than the one-off payment subscription because it includes no discount. The subscription rolls and auto-renews.

QUARTERLY SUBSCRIPTION – This 3 month subscription is paid for upfront by the individual member and features an auto-renewal, as per other subscriptions.

PAY MONTHLY QUARTERLY SUBSCRIPTION – The 3 month subscription is paid for every month and rolls.

MONTHLY SUBSCRIPTION – With this rolling subscription the member pays on a monthly basis, with the subscription renewing automatically every month.

Additionally, free trial conversions feed into this particular subscription.

CORPORATE SUBSCRIPTION

The proposition of the product has the following attributes:

→ **JOBS**
  o Post unlimited jobs
  o 4x featured jobs
  o AI interface
  o Facetted candidate search
  o Manage candidates

→ **NEWS**
  o Product news
  o Company news
  o Industry news
  o Industry diary
  o Industry commentary
  o R&A news
  o Video
  o Collated news
  o Blog
  o Newsletters

→ **GUIDES**
  o How to's
  o Industry guides
  o Salary survey results
  o Standardised job descriptions
  o Career advice articles

→ **COMMUNITY**
  o SEF company profile
  o Browse members
  o Search members

→ **MARKETING**
  o SaaS social media posting
  o SaaS reputation management
  o Resources

→ **R&A**
  o Access to proprietary data sets
  o Access the deals database
  o Access to company profiles (excluding SWOT's)

    o   Access to country-specific industry profiles
    o   Access to survey results
    o   Access to the industry glossary
    o   Ask the expert

The corporate subscription options for this product are limited to:

ANNUAL SUBSCRIPTION – With this subscription the organisation pays upfront for the annual subscription at a reduced price. The subscription then auto-renews every year.

PAY MONTHLY ANNUAL SUBSCRIPTION – This subscription is for a 12 month period, but enables the organisation to pay on a monthly basis. This subscription has a higher yield than the one-off payment subscription because it includes no discount. The subscription rolls and auto-renews.

Web Analytics

Continuous monitoring of performance against targets for any digital business is required. For our example portal business, the analytics can be broken down into the following:

➜ Web analytics
➜ Email campaign monitoring
➜ Social analytics

Depending upon the business model other analytics may be relevant. For most digital businesses however, these will be key.

For example PPC management tools, ad networks and more…

Understanding the Data

Understanding the data is vital. To best understand the data you need to (1) comprehend the numbers and what they mean; (2) compare the numbers against both those predicted in the model and also against the competitive landscape; and (3) understand the drivers of those numbers.

For example, when displaying the top-level stats it is worth highlighting where the numbers are versus target that month. Additionally, how the travel is looking either month-on-month or year-on-year against said target. These are effective KPI's for both the team and/or agency along with the business as a whole.

PLEASE NOTE: Whilst this all sounds rather obvious, it is wise to remember that a few marketers and marketing agencies often play games with numbers and count calendar months and compare to 30 day periods, et cetera.

Standardising the methodology is therefore a good move.

Task Management

This section of the book outlines the typical tasks audience development professionals should undertake on a daily, weekly, or monthly basis.

The tasks themselves are often perfunctory and labour intensive. As a result, methods of automating as many as possible should be found.

As a general rule, I would state a maximum of half a day per week should be dedicated (long-term) to analysis. The remainder of the week should be dedicated purely to growth. Once you have the processes in place, this ratio will happen naturally. Initially though, it will take longer.

<u>Always remember:</u> We are attempting to drive traffic, usage and increase purchases not trying to measure what we have not done. Spend too much time and effort on analysis and you will not achieve the results required for success.

Statistics

Audience development is a vital role for any membership business. The savvy professional should know his/her numbers back to front and upside down. They should know what they want to spend money on. How much money they need to spend, based on the statistics they both write and grok.

Not knowing these numbers is as bad as a CEO not knowing the previous months operating expenditure, or the latest current revenue forecast.

Identifying User Agents and the Team

Whilst the likes of Google Analytics filter out spiders and obviously fake user agents, some will still exist. It is important to filter these out as early in the effort as possible.

Removing IP's and unknown user agents/bots is especially important if you have a specialist website that has a small potential universe of users. Keeping your development team, your office, yourself in there might lead to incorrect data and analysis.

Additionally, it might well be worth the effort to ban IP's that you suspect of causing fraudulent traffic to the website. This can be best implemented on the web server itself, such as Apache. The in-house sys-admin, or external hosting company will be able to assist in this.

Conversion Rates

Each business is going to be different depending upon the variations on proposition and industry. Therefore, rather than state an industry average conversion rate and attempt to benchmark the products against those, instead benchmark the performance against test campaigns carried out during the product development cycle.

Once the team know and understand the performance range possible then experiment with aspects of the sales funnel. Experiment with aspects of the marketing. Also, experiment with aspects of the proposition.

This continued experimentation and A/B/C testing will point the marketer in the right direction.

I see this nimble approach very much as 'hum it; strum it; and then play it properly'. It is designed to increase understanding within the team quickly and efficiently.

Understanding Funnels

A sales funnel within digital media can be defined as steps designed by a business in order to guide its visitors toward a buying decision.

In order to generate sales the business will utilise the principals outlined in the four step AIDA model:

ATTENTION – The often overlooked first step of the model is where the business makes the visitor aware of the products.

INTEREST – Often poor marketers jump straight into this aspect of the AIDA model and ignore the first step and rely upon PPC advertising in order to self-select. –A mistake.

Instead, now the business has the attention of the visitor then it should attempt to persuade and influence that visitor into step three.

DESIRE – The business has attracted a visitor, brought attention to the product and now it must generate desire for access to the product.

This third step, which is also often referred to as 'Decision' is in many ways the most difficult to master for new businesses as they may not yet understand the optimal purchasing decision making process.

ACTION – The success of this portion of the process is often defined not only by the overall strength and tone of the message and proposition, but also by the call to action used to convert the visitor into a customer.

Now we have briefly outlined AIDA and have an understanding as to a sales funnel let us move on to describing the ingredients of a relevant sales funnel in more detail.

Key Components of a Sales Funnel

In this section of the book I will walk you through a typical sales funnel for a membership-based property. I have included options in here for single-copy sales and other potential products, but the aim of the funnel is to maximise subscription sales.

TRAFFIC – Your sales funnel will only ever be successful if you are driving relevant traffic to it. As a result, it is vital that you spend a significant portion of available resource in driving the audience to the property.

It is also vital that you then measure and understand where this traffic is coming from. Doing this merely requires some setup work on Google Analytics, or any other enterprise-class web analytics software you decide to use.

LANDING PAGE – This is the starting point of the funnel and is normally designed purely to motivate the visitor into an action. The layout and functionality of this page should be well researched, with notes taken from successful external products.

Walkthroughs, testimonials and reviews, et cetera can be used, if relevant and if they add strength to the message.

Personally, I like noting the 'Reasons to purchase' on the landing pages. Doing this enables you to immediately explain what the offering is; what problems the platform solves for members; and highlights relevance to the potential user.

EMAIL LIST – It is imperative that you capture as many peoples Email addresses as early in the process as possible.

However, remember what the end game is here. Do not attempt to convolute the offer; add additional forms to pages; or complicate the process. Just a simple lead generator will suffice.

A TRIPWIRE PRODUCT – If the funnel starts with free newsletter or report, then offer a free trial subscription to the website utilising standard tripwire marketing techniques.

For example, the following methodology could be used:

Start by creating a product that will act as a lead magnet. This product could be a free report, or a high quality newsletter. Something that is of good value to the potential customer.

Now create a tripwire product. This could be a time-limited free trial subscription to the platform.

Once you have created your tripwire product then introduce it to the recipients of the free report. You can do this both via Email and via the free report product itself. The aim is to convert all free report recipients into free trial subscribers with the minimum of fuss and as elegantly as possible.

Now, you have converted the free report recipients into time-limited free trial subscribers you need to introduce and then convert them to the main (paid) subscription product. You can do this effectively by both Email, remarketing and by actual usage the product. Remember, the platform utilises a Metered Paywall, so the conversions will likely be largely self-selecting.

As you have probably already realised, the beauty of this model is that the time-limited free trial offer is merely a tripwire version of the main product we are attempting to market.

Analyse, experiment using A/B, or A/B/C testing and then tailor the effort to return the best possible results. This in itself will likely be an ongoing process over the duration of the business lifecycle so take your time and keep moving forward.

THE DOWNSELL PRODUCT – If the potential purchaser abandons the purchase during the process then offer the lead a different, more attractive offer... perhaps a percentage off, or a reduced term membership.

PRODUCT, PLATFORM AND AUDIENCE • 181

You can potentially utilise a well set-up Remarketing campaign to help you here.

SALES PAGE(s) – The sales pages are designed to present and then complete the transaction. They have only one aim and that is to convert the visitor into a customer.

Again, do not complicate. Keep the process as simple and elegant as possible in order to reduce the number of potential subscribers/customers you lose during the transaction.

As with other steps, remember to integrate remarketing campaigns into the source code of the pages.

NETWORKING PAGE – At the end of the registration process an optional page exists where the new registered user can import his/her address book and thus immediately increase the marketing reach of the platform.

How you motivate the new subscriber/customer depends upon the product specification. It could be anything from accessing a complimentary product for free, through to future discounts and free trial offer for friends and/or colleagues.

It is certainly worth your time thinking about how you would motivate the user to help you market in this way.

THANK YOU PAGE – This is (potentially) the last page of the sales funnel and is used as a way of introducing the now subscriber to the product and/or community.

It is however a great page in which to offer a Tripwire product, such as an additional subscription, or product. Brilliant opportunity to upsell additional synergistic products.

Example Sales Funnel

This is an example of a sales funnel for a subscription-based business.

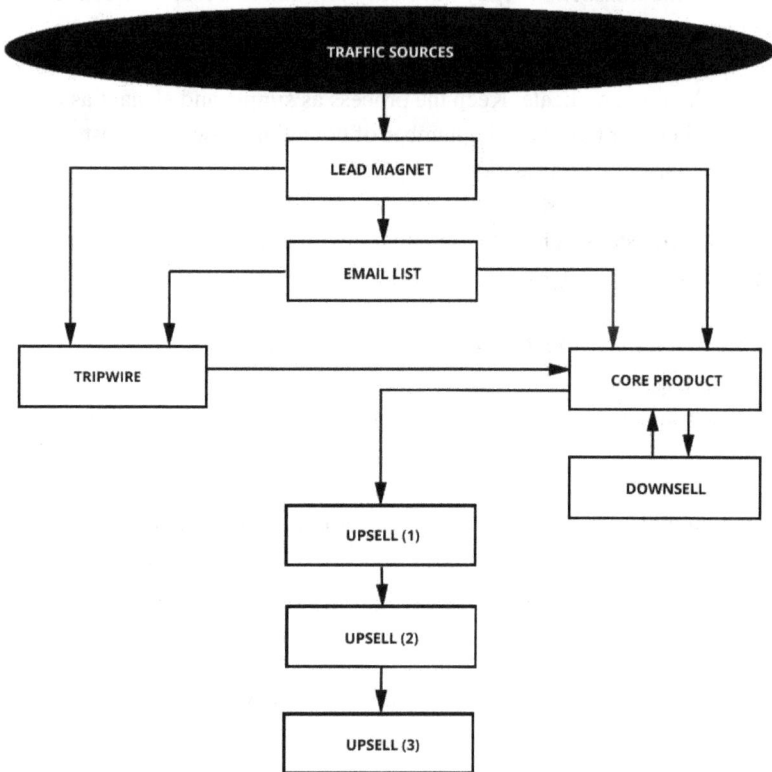

Top-level Email Campaign Statistics

Within the Email broadcasting software the campaign manager will be able to see the results of the relevant campaign.

These results should be gathered no earlier than two full working days after the campaign went out.

Collecting them any earlier than that will reduce the metrics stated… and in-turn impact both the tracking and the KPI's versus industry averages and maybe targets.

The table below highlights the potential success metrics for B2B Email campaigns:

CAMPAIGN	SUCCESS METRICS
ALL OBJECTIVES	Sent; Delivered; Opened; Bounced; Clicks; and CTR
TRAFFIC	Visits to site; Cost per visit
LEADS	Cost per lead; Leads generated; Type of lead
SALES	Conversions; Conversion rate; Average value; ROI; Cost per transaction; Type of sale
UPSALE	Revenue per client pre and post campaign

RENEWAL | Usage generated; Response rate

Social Analytics

Undertaking an ongoing effort to understand and develop your social media presence is important to any marketing effort.

Garner the campaign actuals, measure your performance and then benchmark your performance against (1) your stated competitors in the space; and (2) against defined website types in related industries.

The better software out there will do much of the grunt work for you and create action points that highlight what you need to do in order to compete and improve. The best in class will also offer you a ROI on your efforts across all the major social media channels.

Amongst the most desirable stats to grok are a basic breakdown by social media source; by the time and date of publishing; by number of posts; and also by media type.

The reasoning for the majority of the statistics is fairly obvious and no different to other types of web analytics.

However, the latter is important as the cost of production/effort varies significantly depending upon the content type... and is often overlooked. Knowing and understanding what works on what channel will optimise processes.

Additionally, understanding the sentiment of comments made on your posts to social media channels is important too. As you grow and the figurative snowball starts rolling you will not be able to read each and every comment that is posted on each and every post. Therefore understanding the overall sentiment of these comments will help you better understand your social media audience.

Landing Page Optimisation

The planning process for creating a successful landing page is remarkably simple... and revolves around common sense:

1. **DETERMINE THE PRIMARY OBJECTIVE** – In this case it is to sell a subscription to the portal.

2. **UNDERSTAND THE VISITORS KEY MOTIVATIONS** – How and why are they visiting and (importantly) what will convince them to purchase the subscription

3. **CREATE A LANDING PAGE** – Ensure that is suits points 1 and 2 outlined above, whilst highlighting the value of the product offering

One of the key strategies to use when putting together landing pages for subscription-based products is to highlight the problems you solve. Practically-speaking, these equate to the reasons to purchase.

When listing the reasons to purchase prioritise each bullet point in order of importance and focus on the content and/or functionality that is the most important to the end user. Remember, this is about the end user, not about what is the most expensive to produce, or even most popular.

Remember the mantra – keep it simple, execute well.

PPC Campaigns

PPC is a model of internet marketing pioneered by Goto.com in the 1990's and today remains the most significant driver of revenue for the dominant Search Engine, Google.

At its core the PPC model equates to advertisers paying a fee each time one of their adverts is clicked on. This fee is often defined by the demand for the keyword.

For example, if only one business is bidding on a keyword string such as 'nanotechnology jobs in Australia' then the CPC will be significantly lower than if a keyword string has 100 separate businesses competing for the term 'Jobs in California'.

Within financial services and a number of other highly competitive industries where the ticket price is potentially high the average price for each click is astronomically high. The ROI of the campaigns against these high ticket prices drives this. Sometimes the CPC can reach over $100 per click.

The PPC Effort

Much effort goes into creating and managing effective PPC campaigns.

A campaign effort can be broken down into five simply defined tasks, (1) keyword research, where the marketer defines all the keywords the campaign is to include; (2) creating the advertisement and landing page; (3) managing the finances; (4) campaign optimisation to ensure you are maximising performance and minimising the average CPC; (5) understanding the true ROI for the campaign. In the case of subscription-based businesses, the ROI should best be calculated from the CLV (customer lifetime value).

Agency v In-house Efforts

In terms of the cost of using an agency, you need to consider the following, (1) the set-up time for any/all campaigns; (2) the learning curve required to master your industry; and (3) the margin on the campaign.

Most agencies will charge the equivalent of 10 per cent of the total budget, excluding a set-up fee. The agency will then allocate you an Account Manager based on your value to that business. This account manager may be responsible for setting up the account and even researching the vertical you operate within.

Some agencies however, have knowledgeable staff on the telephones to talk with you as reassurance, yet the actual team managing your account are offshore and have little time to understand your business outside of the budget they have to spend. This is because they are managing multiple clients at the same time.

Additionally, agencies often like to value add to include other marketing services and/or optimisation services. This is especially the case when the agency offers SEO services.

Having originated in marketing and having tried a number of agencies for PPC advertising over the last couple of decades, I believe that any platform-based business needs to be doing the marketing internally.

At the end of the day, if an agency knows your product and industry vertical better than your marketing team then the business will likely fail.

Google AdWords

With a market share of approximately 75 per cent excluding mobile, Google is the most popular Search Engine in the world.

The numbers are staggering. It is estimated that 3.5 billion searches are performed per day by users across the world. That equates to well over a Trillion per year.

With such massive usage, Google is certainly the main player for PPC advertising.

Google has a number of commercial offerings ranging from software access to banners, to remarketing and so on. The primary offering however remains AdWords.

AdWords operates on a PPC model where businesses bid on specific keyword strings and pay for each unique click on the advert they create.

Whenever a person uses Google to search Google matches the keyword string against its AdWords ads. If the advertiser has stipulated within its campaign that this search is relevant then Google will display a select number of AdWords results alongside its organic search results. Whether the advertiser message appears in this list depends not only on the campaign settings they have stipulated, but also the value of the advert to Google.

Google's dominance in the market actually stems from its ability to understand what ads perform the best for its business. Just because an advertiser is bidding the most for a keyword string it does not mean that their advert will display. Google makes the decision automagically by estimating how likely the audience searching for the keyword is to click.

For example, if one business is bidding $1 for a click and another is bidding $1.50, but the advert associated to the $1 campaign will generate 2x clicks against the 1x click for the campaign ad used in the $1.50 campaign then it will display the lower bid first.

Simply put, Google tailors results not on the bid value, but on how much money it will make.

Google Display

Like Google AdWords, Google's Display Network reaches an astonishing number of internet users. Google themselves claim that this reach 90 per cent of the entirety of the internet The network is across millions of web properties as well so targeting for publishers is a dream.

Google's Display Network traditionally costs a little less per visit and is known as being a slightly more passive form of advertising, with a lower ROI. Whereas people searching Google are often looking for something specific, the user of a partner website will likely just be browsing that site.

Google Display advertising is managed through the AdWords platform. Therefore, in order to run display campaigns through Google you will need to have an AdWords account.

For obvious reasons, the key to success for publishers is in the targeting. Whilst you can target by a number of methods, historically I have seen a good deal of success with conversions from banners inventory targeted to appear on B2B-focused properties I know first via managed placements… and then limiting who sees it on those properties.

The targeting types are as follows:

→ Keywords

→ Topic areas
→ Remarketing
→ Managed placements

Once you have the targeting completed and the banners loaded to the platform, the ongoing campaigns will need managing effectively in order to get the most out of them.

Unless your product is aimed at the mass market ignore the high traffic portals and newspaper websites as the traffic available on these properties might hit the demographic and interest area targeting you desire, but the resulting user is likely either not in 'purchasing mode', or maybe merely a person with a passing interest in the subject area. This is especially important for industries such as 'space technology' or 'AI'.

Google Display Network should be a significant player in a B2B industry portals marketing mix.

Facebook

Facebook is a digital goliath with daily active users over 1.4 Billion in 2017. This massive usage translates into nearly $40 Billion in advertising revenue. Revenue that is growing at 49% annually.

The advertising solutions Facebook offers range from promoting posts on your page, traffic to your website, or specific actions on the platform and can be targeted to users based on their location, demographic and the information the user has provided on their profile. The 'Precise interests' and 'Broad categories' targeting are of significant interest to B2B portals like our example business. You would target

Despite the social networks continued focus on native advertising and keeping usage on the platform, it is still possible to send users to external properties.

Once you have create an advert you then set a budget and bid for audience based on the click or CPM methodology.

To get the best performance out of Facebook it is wise to keep a constant (real time) eye on the performance and ROI of campaigns, at least in the initial stages. Unlike Google and therefore Google AdWords, visitors to Facebook are visiting the platform purely to communicate to and catch-up with friends/family/.. This equates to a preselection prior to advertising and means the advertiser needs to spend time tailoring the message to suit.

Having said that, please do not be dissuaded from advertising on the platform if you see a fit. From experience, the overall ROI achievable with Facebook is a match with Google for content-based products.

Instagram

Instagram users tend to be far younger and 'consumer-focused' than that of Facebook. As a result whilst having a foothold on the platform is useful, advertising is probably not massively useful, unless the vertical you are operating within is 'visual' is nature.

If you choose to run campaigns on the platform in order to hit Instagram's demographic then telling a story with your advertising campaign will likely be more successful than standardised advertising messages.

Yahoo Gemini

Yahoo, with its massive usage remains one of the titans of the web.

However, its advertising platform Gemini is perhaps still not as known to marketers as AdWords, or even Bing. On one hand this is an advantage and relatively cheap traffic can be generated.

That said, the CPC of some campaigns on this network is not always as low as you would expect, based on the obviously lower number of active advertisers. One of the reasons for this is that Yahoo have implemented significant quality control over ads, especially within certain verticals and keywords.

Therefore, whilst certainly forming a part of the marketing mix, it is perhaps best to implement PPC campaigns on Google and then Bing before implementing a campaign on Yahoo Gemini. Once successful on those platforms, Yahoo is a good way to grow.

Bing

Whilst far smaller in reach than Google AdWords, advertising on the Bing network arguably offers a greater ROI than with Google AdWords.

The lower level of competition means reduced CPC prices, which along with some very cool dashboard tools enable the marketer to generate healthy campaigns that need less management than AdWords campaigns.

On the negative side, as Bings audience is a mere 10 per cent of Googles the lack of scalability in successful campaigns can be frustrating for marketers. To alleviate this, perhaps scale with another ad network, such as Yahoo Gemini, which offers (somewhat) similar scale to the subscriptions marketer.

YouTube

As mentioned previously in this book, scale of the audience on YouTube is staggering, especially on mobile devices. More than 1.5 Billion people visit the property every month and more than 400 hours of unique content are uploaded to the platform every minute.

Commercially, YouTube offers a low cost video advertising solutions for marketers. Campaigns are set up via the same Google account you use for AdWords. The advertiser can target the user by all the regular categorisations, but with the added bonus of a healthy minimum viewing time before the ad costs money. This has a significant effect on the campaign ROI and as a result makes advertising this channel effective both in terms of numbers and cost.

On the negative side, you have the additional cost of producing an advert that will play well and motivate viewers to join.

Once you have a high quality video prepared then it is worth taking as much time on researching keyword strings and the autocomplete terms on the platform as you would with the other PPC networks. Getting the keywords and title correct will have a massive impact on the both views and overall response rate for the campaign.

Content that is known to work on YouTube includes How To videos, guides, interviews, reviews and summaries. Perhaps tailor the advert to one of these formats and include a call to action overlay offering a free trial subscription to the relevant portal, or free report would be more effective than naively using the medium as a branding exercise.

Other Notable Networks

Below are a couple of additional PPC networks. Although potentially quite weak in Australia, the beauty of these networks is the reduced cost per acquisition.

For example, where the CPC on Google could be $0.75, the equivalent CPC on one of these networks will be significantly less, maybe $0.05.

- → 7SEARCH
- → MILLENNIAL MEDIA
- → INMOBI
- → OUTBRAIN
- → TABOOLA
- → REVCONTENT
- → VIBRANT MEDIA
- → CLICKSOR
- → INFOLINKS

Remarketing

Remarketing, which can also be thought of as retargeting is the practice of setting a cookie in the users browser in order to have an advertisement follow that user around the web after they have left the website, or page where the cookie was originally set.

It is recommended that if you use Google AdWords, Google Display Network and Facebook Ads then you should also use Google Remarketing. Implementing a campaign here will likely bring your cost per acquisition numbers down.

The following diagram outlines the remarketing process:

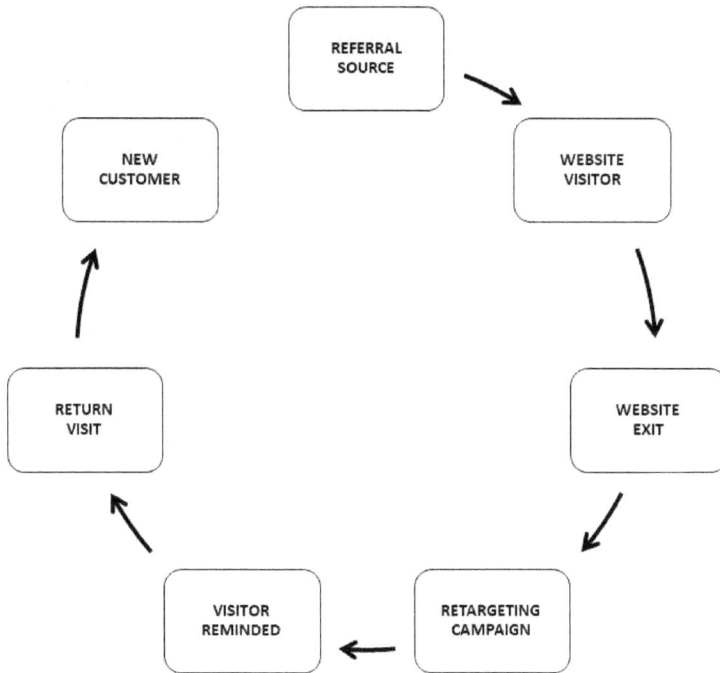

Other notable retargeting networks may, or may not be relevant to your portal business. These include:

→ CHANGOO
→ ADROLL
→ FACEBOOK
→ CHANGO
→ PERFECT AUDIENCE
→ TRIGGIT
→ RETARGETER

SEO

Most Search Engines are commercial businesses. They have two types of results, which are often presented on the same page:

1. **ORGANIC RESULTS** – The first is organic, whereby the search engine presents the person searching with results based on what it deems the most relevant web page available.

2. **PAID RESULTS** – The second is the results that businesses pay for... and how the search engine makes money.

    In the 21st century the model has become far more detailed and nuanced, but on a rudimentary basis, the paid results are actioned using an ongoing auction process where the business paying the most amount of money has the privilege of presenting their advert to the person searching.

Search Engine Optimisation (SEO) relates solely to the organic listings that appear on SERP's.

The (partial) Myth of SEO

When I first started my journey back in mid-1996, I owned an SEO business... one of the first in the UK. I was entirely self-trained in the dark arts, learning very much through trial and error because of a sudden and unexpected requirement to sell soft toys and collectables for a family-owned craft centre.

I learnt a lot during those early pre-Google days. Everything from architecture and development on the LAMP stack for increasing relevance on Search Engines through to e-commerce and the rest.

My SEO business worked with many web design and development agencies who at the time were just cottoning on to the potential of the web as a medium for 'selling'. They loved what we could do for them. We got them results; and achieved them fast.

To speak frankly, half the time all we really had to do was boost the volume of quality links the site had; ensure that the metatags were optimised; and that the content of the page was as relevant and keyword rich as each search engine allowed. If that wasn't possible, then we'd create a 'gateway' page for them to achieve the same result. We enjoyed great success, especially with AltaVista.

Since those heady days though, many things have changed. The landscape has become crowded with the majority of SEO agencies pushing clients to spend big on 'keyword research', which whilst useful, is not exactly what I would call search engine optimisation, per se. The agencies utilise tools and subscribe to the latest and greatest SaaS platforms promising advantage. The end results for the vast majority of clients are always the same. Why, exactly is that?

The answer is simple, SEO has evolved into little more than analytics and research. It achieves little in the way of tangible results; lacks any real transparency; and is performed by the most junior members of the marketing team. It seems every marketing team, especially within the publishing sector now has a resident 'SEO guru'. As for the agencies...

Staff read blogs on the subject and take the writings of these talented and professional journalists as gospel, seemingly unaware that the writer has no notable success, or indeed experience in the field. If a manager at Google said it; if a writer at xyz.com wrote it, then it simply must be true.

White Hat SEO is good, we are told this by the experts' who's advice gets regurgitated throughout the internet economy by those game-fully employed in the industry. Black Hat is bad. Terrible. You'll get banned.

Actually, you probably will get banned. It's just a matter of time. When an entire industry is dependent upon one vehicle for its breakfast, lunch and dinner you best play fair and by the rules.

What if post development SEO was a complete waste of time and money and the White Hat SEO that the industry, Google and the rest push actually died about a decade ago.

Fact is, it is very difficult and exceptionally rare for a junior search engine optimiser to have much of an effect on the performance of a website, after the website has been developed. The web just doesn't work that way anymore.

Having said all of that, the search engine optimiser can certainly still have an impact during the development of the property, to ensure that guidelines, redirects, SEF links, et alai are all done correctly.

Sad, but true.

Understanding On-page and Off-page SEO

Search Engine Optimisation consists of two aspects, On-page SEO and Off-page SEO.

The easiest way to describe the difference between the two aspects is that Off-page SEO is all garnering authority from across the web for your targeted keyword term, or string; whilst On-page SEO is about improving the relevance of your page to the keyword term, or string in the Search Engine.

On-page SEO

The main ingredients on on-page SEO are as follows:

- → Create a valid SEF link structure for the portal
- → Include important keywords in URL's where possible
- → Use Meta Title, Meta Description tags within the source code
- → Optimise the Meta Title tag to include the desired keywords
- → Optimise the Meta Description tag to explain the web page utilising keywords, where possible
- → Build a relationship between the Meta Title, Meta Description, URL and actual title of the article
- → Start each content item with a preferred keyword, or keyword string
- → Wrap the title of each content item in a H1 tag
- → Prioritise keywords in the first third of the page.
- → Exclude keywords from the bottom third of the web page
- → Use permanent links
- → Utilise web standards
- → Create clean code
- → Improve load speed
- → Minimise external links
- → Control total number of links on each page
- → Ensure each page has unique content
- → Create a sitemap
- → Encourage Search Engines to crawl the website
- → Minimise broken links
- → Have a responsive web design
- → Attempt to have a balanced text to code ratio

Additionally, you may want to:

➜ Minimise social bookmarking links
➜ Sculpt internal links
➜ Include a publishing date

Now we have looked at on-page SEO, let us discuss at off-page SEO and areas where marketers and audience development professionals can have a tangible impact within a 3-4 month period.

Off-page SEO

In-short, off-page SEO relates to all the various activities you undertake around the Internet, excluding those on your own domain to boost the relevance of the website for targeted keywords on Search Engines.

These activities normally consist of the following:

➜ Link building
➜ Social bookmarking
➜ Directory submission
➜ Content marketing
➜ Comments
➜ Forum entries
➜ Video posts

The following sections of the book look in considerably more detail on the art of link building, social media posting and more.

LINK BUILDING

As part of any SEO strategy it is vitally important to increase the number (and maximize the quality) of incoming links.

TARGET .EDU DOMAINS

As part of any SEO campaign, it is vitally important to get links from relevant websites. The higher the relevance to the page you are getting the link from then the greater the relevance score attributed to the page.

Education establishments are especially important with this as Google and others see them as non-commercial entities and therefore a link is not tainted by commercial requirements.

Remember, just one .EDU, or .GOV link is worth 5-10 high quality links, despite what some 'SEO experts' claim.

The reasoning behind this additional value is the fact that Search Engines see .EDU and .GOV links as being untainted by commercial pressures. This means that when they index the page they see it as a genuine endorsement of the contextual value and relevance of the page being linked to.

ASKING FOR A LINK

Perhaps the most subtle and effective way to "ask" for a link is to find some ultra-relevant content on the site being promoted... content that the site in question would want to link to. After all, this is exactly what the Search Engines consider the intended use for links.

Find an article and then send an Email to the webmaster of the target site essentially saying something like the following:

Hi First Name,

I am writing from XYZ and wanted to inform you of an article we recently wrote on XYZ. I think you might find quite interesting as %INSERT_REASON_HERE%.

If you want to check it out, you can find it here: http://www.xyz.com.

I'd appreciate any feedback you have.

Kind regards,
My Name

With this approach there is a good chance they will look at the article and, if they like it, write about it and/or link through to it. When writing this type of correspondence it helps to be specific, introduce yourself as a regular reader of their site/blog and (importantly) contextually relate the content item you are promoting to theirs.

This method is especially effective if you can create a piece of content relevant to a recent topic, or discussion (either on or offline) in your subject area or a recent article by the individual you're requesting a link from. It should no longer seem surprising that relevant, topical, quality content is the most effective way to get quality links.

Putting it in front of the right eyes just helps the process.

RULES OF ENGAGEMENT

As the marketing person surfs the web for potential links, they'll often run up against sites where link acquisition can be difficult. If the site doesn't provide a clear path to getting a link, don't be discouraged, there are a variety of tactics you can employ, including:

SEARCH FOR OTHER OUTBOUND LINKS – If you can find a page on the site that's linking out to other relevant sites, either as advertising or direct referral, you can generally use that as a good entryway to your link acquisition.

When you call or Email, mention your interest in being listed on that page along with their other outbound links – you can offer a trade in services, direct payment or pitch the value of your content

LOOK FOR AN ADVERTISING PAGE – Any page that lists a contact for advertising or affiliates is ripe for targeting. Be prepared to pay for these types of links, as they are almost always part of a site's monetization strategy.

CHECK FOR A BLOG – Blogs are excellent sources for links, and can often be pitched with content (discussed in the next section)

LOCATE A RELEVANT EMAIL ADDRESS – Emails for sales contacts and support are not nearly as helpful as website managers, webmasters and directors of online operations or, in many cases, business owners.

You need to find someone who has decision-making authority about the content of the website, which in many cases requires an owner (in the event of a small business) or a manager in larger companies

CALL – There's no harm in calling whatever phone numbers you can find, asking to be routed to the person who handles website content or website advertising and making your case

BE FRIENDLY AND PERSISTANT – Many times when making link requests, you'll get initial pushback (from un-returned telephone calls and

Emails to flat-out negative responses). Your best move in these cases is to be as genuine and affable as possible and search for a way for to have the site owners make you an offer

The practice of finding a link contact can be arduous, but over time, you'll become more and more familiar with the format of websites in your industry. Depending on how valuable or important you consider the link to be, it can be worth a good deal of time and energy to negotiate an acquisition.

Social Media Marketing

The entire population of the world currently stands at a 7.5 Billion, or so. Out of these people, a massive 3.5 Billion have access to the internet through a computer, tablet, or smartphone. From this, more than 2.25 Billion people use social media.

Whatever your horizontal, or vertical industry. Whatever your demographic, social media offers a unique access point to your target market, be they audience, potential member, or even business client.

As a membership-based business it is absolutely vital that the company has an effective, optimised social media marketing and engagement strategy.

It has been widely acknowledged for the past 5-6 years that social media has overtaken SEO in terms of priority within the content marketing paradigm.

Before you start marketing products and platforms to social media it is important to understand the differences between the various platforms.

These differences include fundamentals such as its users and in how these users actually utilise the platform.

For example, Facebook is aimed people looking for news and comment from their friends and acquaintances.

Twitter, on the other hand despite its newly increased character count is still all about immediate and about speedy interactions. It is a key driver of the news cycle, especially within the cultural and current affairs portion of news.

Pinterest and Instagram are great for visual storytelling, but dominated by lifestyle, celebrity, or narcissism-related content. Somewhat irrelevant for our example emerging technology portal business.

For a portal business aimed at professionals working within stipulated industry verticals, LinkedIn will likely be amongst the most useful social media platforms.

This book spends some time on strategies you could use to maximise your potential on this network.

Additionally, this section offers outlines various strategies that should be undertaken across the entirety of social media.

Twitter

Twitter is a great way of garnering targeted attention for the portals; and a method of driving what I like to describe as diverse traffic. Jobs-based traffic, news-based traffic; offer-based traffic. Lots of potentials to generate new users and subscribers.

The cost of advertising on Twitter depends upon a number of factors, including the advertising type.

For example, the price will be different for a campaign aimed at increasing your followers on the platform than it will be for driving traffic to the website, or app.

Twitter has three main methods of advertising:

1. **PROMOTED TWEETS** – This is where the advertiser promotes a specific tweet to a demographic of choice over a set period of time.

2. **PROMOTED TRENDS** – This form of advertising enables businesses to promote a trend and put the story to the top of the list for a specific time period.

3. **PROMOTED PROFILES** – Using this method, the advertiser can invite other Twitter users to follow their account. This is one of the better (paid) ways in which to grow your followers.

In terms of cost, the average CPM for Twitter is significantly higher than that of Facebook... with a lower average value per visitor. The CTR however, is far better and Twitter are quickly becoming more competitive.

Instagram

Whilst not deemed as 'serious' or vital to B2B as a LinkedIn, Twitter, or Facebook, Instagram is more important than you might initially think. Its traffic is growing at an increasing rate, which mirrors the growing usage patterns you see with other very visual platforms such as YouTube.

As a result, below are a few key tactics you can use to grow your audience and impact on Instagram worth considering.

ENGAGEMENT PODS – As mentioned elsewhere in this book Engagement Pods are a new phenomenon and involves fellow members of the community agreeing to promote each other's posts. This is an artificial method of boosting the relevance and ranking of posts within the Instagram platform.

Whether Instagram will attempt to outlaw these pods remains to be seen. It is however

INFLUENCER MARKETING – Again, we look at this in slightly more detail elsewhere within the book. In-short, if the niche publisher can partner informally, or formally with an influencer within the target space then the attention that that 'influencer' garners for the business is huge.

For example, I am sure you could you imagine how much a link from the likes of Elon Musk would be worth to a publisher operating within the space tech sector. The increase in gravitas and exposure would be hugely important to that business.

BOOSTING POSTS – It will be worthwhile boosting relevant Instagram posts in order to maximise the potential of the important posts. This is especially the case with the more valuable 'evergreen' content; or with content that you want to utilise in order to draw visitors into the sales funnel.

PROFILE PAGE – The importance of the Instagram profile page is growing, especially for brands.

STORIES – Instagram has a stories-based advertising platform. This offers publishers a massively increased opportunity to access and convert relevant users.

LinkedIn

Below are some tips for using LinkedIn posts to generate traffic.

Firstly, it is vital to note that you do not need tens of thousands of company followers to have your post seen by hundreds of thousands of relevant users.

In fact, all you actually have to do is write good content and follow a number of rules and steps, listed below. These are key tips to going viral on that platform:

LINE LENGTH – It has been acknowledged that on social media line length plays a role in the likelihood of an audience reading it. Whilst you can easily see this as a dumbing down of society due to poor attention spans, the science remains very real. Basically keep the paragraphs short and snappy.

Additionally, ensure that each paragraph looks visually attractive. In the real world this equates to one sentence in the first paragraph, two sentences in the second, one sentence in the third and perhaps three sentences in the next.

The aim with this is to create what is known as wave pattern writing.

FIND A HOOK – this is standard for both journalism and marketing communications so the team should already be doing this.

POST OFTEN – Have a routine and build relationships with your users.

DO NOT INCLUDE A LINK IN THE MAIN BODY OF YOUR POST – The reasoning behind this is that LinkedIn is in the business of trying to keep users on its platform. LinkedIn, for obvious reasons hates losing a user to external websites so will penalise any and all posts that contain links within them.

Instead of posting the link in the post, post it in the first comment. – Frequent users of LinkedIn will notice this trend in most posts that gain significant traction and likes.

NEVER INCLUDE GRAPHICS – If you include photos, images, or even infographics in your post, the algorithm will deduct points.

LinkedIn currently does not read content hidden within photos so automagically marks them down

DO NOT MENTION CITIES – If you mention your location anywhere in the post, it will likely impact the targeting of the post... with LinkedIn deeming it more relevant to that city than anywhere else. Basically, you will limit your audience to that city.

TELL A STORY – Remember to have a beginning, middle and end.

UTILISE ENGAGEMENT PODS – I have written more information on Engagement Pods in a related section of this document.

SPONSORED UPDATES

LinkedIn Sponsored Updates enable a content producer to drive leads by publishing directly to the feed, where members engage with content.

One of the key benefits to using the platform is that you can reach the right audience using comprehensive targeting, such as job title and function, seniority, industry, company, geography, education, et cetera. The message can be read on every device in any number of formats, including video.

In terms of financials, the business model they employ is Cost per Click, or Cost per Impression. Whilst more expensive than Facebook and Google, it would likely be an effective method of generating paid or free trials subscriptions for the business.

LINKEDIN ADVERTISING SOLUTIONS

LinkedIn is a great way of targeting potential subscribers.

The solution works in a similar way to the old version of Facebook feeds. Business users can publish updates and target users by a number of criteria.

To get started update the company page on the platform with new content. Once you have done that, then sponsor that content and target the audience by location, company, job title/description, skillset, education and a lot, lot more. Then simply set the bid amount using the CPC or CPM methodologies. Launch the campaign and then measure the engagement metrics.

You can choose Email, banners, and text as the unit with this type of advertising.

Again, advertising on LinkedIn is more expensive then Facebook, or Google, but will likely prove a valuable tool in your subscription marketing arsenal.

LINKEDIN COMPANIES PAGE

It is wise to firstly ensure that the company page is fully set-up and that all members of staff are listed and up to date.

Once this task has been completed then write a catchy company blurb as journalists will often use this page as a source.

Please note that special attention needs to be paid to company listings where a number of staff are listed under one entity, whilst others are listed under another.

LINKEDIN GROUPS

It is important to join the most relevant LinkedIn groups.

For example, there are a number of LinkedIn groups aimed at the nanotechnology industry. Joining, immersing yourself within and networking with members of these groups is an important p way of reaching your target market.

Some tips for maximising potential here include:

RULES – Understand the posting and commenting rules on LinkedIn

SEARCH – Find the correct people by searching for the keywords that matter to you.

For example, it will be far more effective to base your targeting around relevant vertical industries and/or organisations and not around horizontal job titles

VALUE – Grok the quality of the discussions taking place and decide what value and tone you can add to the conversation

CONNECT – Grow the number of connections. With LinkedIn, it is imperative that you have as many 1st and 2nd level connections. Take some time to increase your follower count

PROFESSIONALISM – Stay calm and be patient. Do not jump straight in and start spamming the group with subscription offers

Remember, this is a network of incredibly relevant people. Treat them like gold dust... and take your time by offering as much value to them as you can. Better still, act as a guide for the industry

ACTIVITY – Be active. Be consistent. Always be consistently active

〰〰〰〰〰〰〰〰〰〰〰〰〰〰〰〰〰〰〰〰〰

Google+

Similar to many other social networks, Google+ can be a useful content and business marketing tool, especially for niche publishers.

Firstly, it should be noted that each URL created using Google+ is included in Google SERP's and as a result creates a potential entry point to your business.

Secondly, Google as a platform has an incredible amount of traffic and functionality. Google+ sits within the platform and integrates well with other areas of the Google Empire.

Hangouts are one hugely relevant example here. Editorial teams can use Hangouts and Google+ as a great mechanism to interact with potential users.

Thirdly, and perhaps most interestingly, Google+ is a social network based around interests rather than pre-existing relationships. This is vital and great for building new audiences within our example portals target industry verticals.

StumbleUpon

StumbleUpon is a good source of cheap (and free) traffic. Its relevance to emerging technology sectors is obvious as it has targeted interest areas and demographics that precisely match the target market for all the sites. However, these interest areas will not necessarily mean professionals working within the sector.

To target those then you must utilise the paid advertising model and target the correct demographics. It will obviously not be perfect, but the relevancy will be increased.

PAID

The average CPC for a targeted StumbleUpon visitor is $0.15. This is actually relatively decent value as you can target nicely and they guarantee that the visitor stays on the property for a minimum period of time (15 seconds, I believe).

Scale-wise, StumbleUpon is also quite capable of sending a few thousand relevant visitors to your property on a daily basis. The average page views per visitor is as competitive as Google PPC and Facebook Ads.

FREE

Free traffic from Stumble is great, but of significantly lower quality than the paid version.

During my career I have had days where it was beaten only by Drudge Report, Twitter, Facebook and Google as a source of visitors. Basically, more traffic than Yahoo and Bing combined.

Other Social Bookmarking Properties

Social Bookmarking is a genre of website where the user can share a webpage, video, or list that they found interesting/useful. The resident audience on the social bookmarking sites are then presented with these items, which are categorised by tag, via a folksonomy, or by a pre-defined taxonomical list.

The main social bookmarking website out there are StumbleUpon, Pinterest (which is also defined as a social network), Reddit and Digg.

A myriad of social bookmarking site exist, ranging in quality from Slashdot, which is an editorial-driven website... and highly relevant to our example portal business, through to the thousands of Pligg-based websites out there.

Here is a list of a few of the larger sites you could categorise as social bookmarking websites:

- → REDDIT
- → SCOOP.IT
- → POCKET
- → DIGG
- → DELICIOUS
- → DRIBBLE
- → NEWSVINE
- → FOLKD
- → BIZSUGAR
- → DZONE

Wikipedia

It is important that all properties to be featured on Wikipedia.

Wikipedia will only accept new Wiki entries on businesses, or people that are heavily cited around the web in national newspapers, or other trusted information sources.

Instead, concentrate on getting Wikipedia page created for all the businesses web properties and ensure that any and all information included on the page are cited.

To successfully complete the task, you need to ensure that it is not done (1) within the office, as the IP will identify the writer of the Wiki page as biased; (2) ensure at least 4x citations; (3) make the page include at least 250 words; and (4) ensure that the user writing the page(s) has a history of creating and/or editing content on Wikipedia.

In terms of each site, Wikipedia will be both a sizeable direct and indirect source of traffic.

The editors at Wikipedia state that links in the encyclopaedia links do not equate to SERP's on Google. However, if you believe this is the case, then I have a bridge to sell you.

Email

For digital properties operating in the membership economy, Email remains a key way in which to generate new subscriptions and inform existing members.

Emailing your list is a fundamentally cost effective way of generating sales. However, the list is precious and should not be abused by overuse and/or offer a confused message. Great care should be taken to ensure that the minimum number of messages are sent per month… and that all messages have the correct permissions in place.

To run an Email campaign you will need to find some broadcasting software such as MailChimp, or Cheetah Mail. These broadcasting services will for a low cost manage the lists automagically for you.

Testing the Variables

The following variables should be tested during Email campaigns:

VARIABLE	DESCRIPTION
THE LIST	Current subscribers, or lapsed members, or leads
BROADCAST TYPE	What kind of Email was it? Newsletter, Email promotion, News Alert, Usage Summary, Account information, Job Alert, et cetera
CONTACT FREQUENCY	The last time the contact was contacted by Email, SMS, phone, postal, et alia
DEMOGRAPHIC	Location, Age, Gender, Education, Job Title, Horizontal Categorisation
SEGMENT	Know your membership. Know your potential membership. Know your customer. Know your potential customer.

THE OFFER	What offer is going out? What are the actual terms of the individual offer?
CREATIVE	HTML, or Text?
LANDING PAGE	Where are the folk clicking on the campaign landing? The homepage? The product page? The designated landing/conversion page?
SUBJECT LINE	What is the subject of the Email broadcast?
RESPONSE TYPE	How did the customer respond? Via Email, SMS, telephone?
DATE/TIME	When did the Email go out? Note the approximate broadcast time and remember staggered broadcasting is likely.
RESPONSE TIME	When did the recipient, click, or respond in any way?
TEMPLATE	Which Email template did you use?
USER LOG	When was the list member signed up? When did they last use the property?
BEHAVIOUR	Has the user purchased a subscription? What type?

Free Reports

Each portal our example business will operate will produce at least one free report and then market it to visitors not only to the portal, but also to the traffic drivers of the portal.

The purpose of creating a free report is to encourage potential visitors to visit the property and input contact information in order to receive high value, hard to get data. Information that they, as professionals working within the particular sector desire.

Free Report Functionality

The free report functionality has two simple aims, (1) to capture user information; and (2) to enable that user to then pick up a link to the report that they can then download.

It is important to make this a link rather than merely forwarding the form submission page on to the report itself, as you will have the excuse in the users' eye to capture his/her details.

The download form features the minimum number of form fields. Only collect what is absolutely necessary as for every additional action and/or field you will lose potential leads.

➔ Full name
➔ Job title
➔ Company
➔ Email
➔ Telephone
➔ Checkbox (for newsletter subscription)

~~~~~~

Free Report Production

The free report needs to be of sufficient value to your audience so as to motivate the visitor to complete the form.

In order to meet this perceived value requirement some thought needs to be placed into the subject matter… and its relationship with your paid offerings, such as the subscription products.

The free report itself could be created either internally, or by an outside (offshore) agency. If producing the report externally assume $2,500 for the production of it in either India, or the Philippines.

Reports that work best are (1) visual in nature; (2) data-driven, perhaps from survey results; and (3) contain genuinely hard to find, problem-solving information.

~~~~~~

Free Report Marketing

The free report should be advertised on PPC advertising channels, social media and via the website. Concentrate on the subject matter and add things like the keyword "paper", "report", "update", et cetera. You want people to download the report so that you can capture the person's relevant information.

In terms of the marketing materials, it would be worth looking at explaining the following:

➜ Who its aimed at
➜ Why they need to download it

→ Value – do not be shy from attributing a monetary value to the information
→ Make the report time sensitive so as to motivate usage (urgency)
→ Use click colours such as red or orange on the download button

In addition to this, it is always worth allowing the visitor to see a mock-up of the report.

This can be done either as presenting the information as a book, or in report format.

Nanotechnology
Industry Brief

Banners

The commercial model involved with banner advertising can be broken down into the following:

→ Cost Per Click (CPC)
→ Cost Per Impression (CPM)
→ Cost Per Acquisition (CPA)
→ Daily/Weekly/Monthly Fee
→ Inventory swap

In terms of achievable ROI, expect an average CTR of between 0.05 per cent and 0.1 per cent for a correctly targeted campaign. You can improve the potential by utilising video and other rich media formats, but the highest CTR you are likely to receive is about 0.3 per cent.

Globally, the most popular advertising units sold are as follows:

➔ Large Rectangle (336x280 pixels)
➔ Square (250x250 pixels)
➔ Skyscraper (120x600 pixels)
➔ Wide Skyscraper (160x600 pixels)
➔ Half Page Ad (300x600 pixels)
➔ Standard Banner (468x60)

Ad Networks

Networks selling inventory of different types are common and based upon demographics, locale, or upon industry. Below is a list of just some of the networks out there:

➔ SOVRN
➔ DISTRICT M
➔ BREALTIME
➔ PULSEPOINT
➔ SITESCOUT
➔ EXPONENTIAL
➔ IDG TECHNET
➔ ROCKETFUEL
➔ IGNITIONONE
➔ ADVERTISING.COM
➔ ADKNOWLEDGE
➔ EPOM
➔ YAHOO!
➔ PROPEL MEDIA (AKA TRAFFICVANCE)
➔ VIEWBOX
➔ ADROLL
➔ BOOKBUB
➔ IDG NET

➔ 33 ACROSS
➔ VERTOX
➔ INDEX ECHANGE
➔ AMAZON PUBLISHER SERVICES
➔ OPENX
➔ MEDIA.NET
➔ DEFY MEDIA
➔ 152 MEDIA
➔ DOUBLECLICK AD EXCHANGE
➔ COMMISSION FACTORY
➔ ADBLADE
➔ BUYSELLADS
➔ MIDROLL
➔ FAMEBIT
➔ TRAFFICJUNKY
➔ JUICYADS

- → ADSTERRA
- → REVENUE HITS
- → UNDERTONE
- → BIDVERTISER
- → MEDIA NEXUS
- → HAXHAX

- → ADXPANSION
- → PROPELLER ADS
- → BLOG ADS
- → PULSE POINT
- → CONVERSANT

Content Marketing

Often (unfairly) frowned upon, one content marketing method to consider is to pay AU$1,000 for an article to be written and (guaranteed to be) featured on one of the main publishing websites, such as Huffington Post (US), CNN, Buzzfeed, Forbes, Inc, TechCrunch, et cetera.

This kind of content marketing activity is often worth a punt… as if successful then the benefits are many.

Forums

It is vital that the team post content to relevant forums and bulletin boards. The number of boards out there is enormous and finding one with viable relevance to the product/service offered is likely. Therefore picking a few of these boards and posting a link to the article would improve the opportunity for the article to be read by more interested parties.

Like Directories, a high quality forum also not only drives traffic, but also drives the drivers of traffic. Increasing the number of relevant links for the site on relevant properties is a hugely important task… and one best undertaken by those that understand the segment.

Any posts should not be marketing per se and should relate to the subject being posted. Successful forum posting is about immersing yourself in to the community and not (repeat NOT) visibly marketing. Your marketing could simply be including a link to your content in your signature.

Google News

It is important to talk to Google and get each property included in the Google News crawls. If an article is featured prominently on Google News then it can increase the volume of traffic reaching a website by thousands.

The addition of a Metered Paywall enables Google to feature the content without marking is as 'subscriber only', which will downplay its relevance and minimise the number of people clicking on the links.

Other News Websites

Below is a list of news Search Engines and properties that it will be worth submitting the homepage and/or newsfeed to:

→ NEWS NOW
→ ALL BUSINESS
→ 1ST HEADLINES
→ ALTERNET
→ ALTWEEKLIES
→ EIN
→ CRAYON

→ NEWS IS FREE
→ NEWS BLAZE
→ NEWSER
→ NEWSEUM
→ NEWS LIBRARY
→ NEWS MAX
→ WOWOWOW

→ E-NEWSWIRES
→ HEADLINE SPOT
→ JOURNALISM.ORG
→ LEXIS NEXIS / MOREOVER

→ YAHOO NEWS (VIA SUPPLIERS)
→ GOOD GOPHER
→ NEWSLOOKUP

It is likely that you will see a number of additional industry-specific properties to submit your site to. Certainly, with regard to the books example nanotechnology portal I quickly spotted twenty other science-oriented properties that would be worth submitting the website to.

RSS Search Engines and Directories

Below is a list of directories and Search Engines it will be worth submitting the RSS feeds to:

→ ALLTOP.COM
→ BLOGARAMA.COM
→ ALLFORBLOG.COM
→ BLOGCATALOG.COM
→ BLOG-COLLECTOR
→ BLOGDIGGER.COM
→ TWINGLY.COM
→ RSSMICRO.COM
→ FEEDCAT.NET
→ FEEDAGE.COM
→ RSS-NETWORK.COM

→ RSSMOTRON.COM
→ PLAZOO.COM
→ FEEDLISTING
→ NEWZALERT.COM
→ FEEDAGG.COM
→ BLOGADR.COM
→ FEEDPLEX.COM
→ FEEDMAILER.NET
→ FEEDSEE.COM
→ XMETA.NET
→ FEEDGY.COM

Blog Directories and Search Engines

You should submit the site to any appropriate blog and/or RSS feed directories. At worst, it provides a few benign links and helps people find you more easily. At best, you can get tremendous exposure on popular directories like Technorati, Google Blog Search, and Bloglines.

Below is a list of the major blogging directories I compiled 2-3 years ago for a project I was working on:

- 2RSS
- 5STARBLOGS
- ADDYOURBLOG
- ALL-BLOGS.NET
- ANSWERS
- AVIVA
- BLAWG
- BLLOGGS
- BLOGARAMA
- BLOGBIB
- BLOGBUNCH
- BLOGCATALOG
- BLOGCODE
- BLOG-COLLECTOR
- BLOGDIGGER
- BLOGDIR
- BLOG-DIRECTORY
- BLOGGERNOW
- BLOGEXPLOSION
- BLOGFLU
- BLOGGAPEDIA
- EATONWEB
- FEEDAGE
- FEEDBOY
- FEEDNUTS
- FEEDSFARM
- FEEDZA
- FINDINGBLOG
- FYBERSEARCH
- GLOBEOFBLOGS
- GOBIGNETWORK
- IBLOG DIR
- ICEROCKET
- LSBLOGS
- NEWSGATOR
- PLAZOO
- EATONWEB
- POSTAMI
- PRESSRADAR
- RATEITALL
- READABLOG
- REDTRAM

- → BLOGGERNITY
- → BLOGHOP
- → BLOGHUB
- → BLOGINTRO
- → BLOGLINES
- → BLOGPULSE
- → BLOGS.COM
- → BLOG-SEARCH
- → BLOGS-COLLECTION
- → BLOGSCHOLAR
- → BLOGVILLE
- → BLOGZ
- → BOINGBOING
- → BOTW BLOG DIRECTORY
- → BULLETIZE
- → CHORDATA
- → CONTENTSMATTER
- → DIARIST
- → REGATOR
- → SCIENCEPORT
- → SEARCH4RSS
- → SMALL BUSINESS BLOG DIRECTORY
- → SMALLBUSINESS
- → STRATEGIC BOARD
- → SYNDIC8
- → TAILRANK
- → TECHNORATI
- → THEVITAL
- → TODAY
- → TOPIX
- → TRUTHLAIDBEAR
- → WILSDOMAIN
- → WINGEE
- → YAHOO

Co-registrations

A co-registration marketing scheme is where a website collects data (normally standard registration information) from its users as and when they sign-up and then shares this information with its partners.

The way that this is normally done is via an opt-in box that visitors are motivated to check during the registration process. This is normally a special offer.

Vendors within the alcoholic beverages industry in the UK pioneered this kind of marketing to great effect back in the early part of this century.

The normal commercial model for 'co-reg' is based on CPL, with the value depending upon (1) the type of data available; (2) and the quality and quantity of data; (3) the format of the data; and (4) the value of the user demographic, industry, purchasing power, or interest area.

Just about any publishing business could utilise a co-registration campaign with non-competitive properties. With just a bit of savvy planning and effective targeting the business may experience a good take-up rate of free subscriptions.

Job Boards

As the business will be utilising a Metered Paywall, it opens up the opportunity to cross-post jobs on the various job-based Search Engines either using a paid system like Broadbean, or simply providing the partner website with an XML feed of the jobs.

This strategy could be a transformational traffic driver for the network.

Below is a list of just some of the job boards that could take the feed and forward traffic to the various websites:

- → 1JOB
- → 247 JOBS
- → 4 UK JOBS
- → 4SCIENCEJOBS.COM
- → 4TEACHINGJOBS
- → AAIR
- → AALAS
- → ACCESS-SCIENCE JOBS
- → ACS

- → BUBBLE
- → CAD JOBS
- → CAMPAIGN
- → CANADA IT
- → CAREER BOARD
- → CAREER BUILDER
- → CAREER JET
- → CAREER POST
- → CAREER WEB

- AD VIEW
- ADZUNA
- ALL EXEC JOBS
- AOCS
- APA
- APPLYNOW
- ASA
- ASBMB
- ASCB
- ASM CAREER CONNECTIONS
- AUSTJOBS.COM
- BCS
- BETABANEN
- BI JOBS
- BIOSPACE
- BIOTECHNOLOGY JOBS
- BLUESTEPS
- BRIGHT RECRUITS
- BRITISH JOBS
- INDEED.CO.AU
- INDEED.CO.UK
- GIGAJOB
- HALLO
- INDEED.COM
- IOP
- JOBS IN PHARAM
- JOBSERVE
- JOOF
- JORA
- MEDZILLA
- MITULA
- MONSTER
- MYPHARMA
- CAREERHUB
- CAREERS GLOBAL
- CAREERS IN CYBER
- CCL
- CDF ONLINE
- CIC
- CLEARLY IT
- COM JOBS
- COMPILER JOBS
- CONSULTANTHUB
- ECONSULTANCY
- EU JOBS
- EXECUTIVES ON THE WEB
- FDN
- FIND EMPLOYMENT
- FIND EMPLOYMENT
- GENOMEWEB
- GEOSCIENCE
- HIRE LIFE SCIENCE
- ICRUNCH DATA
- IFT
- GLOSJOBS
- GREEN ENERGY JOBS
- GREENJOBS
- SCIENCE CAREER SITE
- SIMPLY HIRED
- SOLAR JOBS
- SOT
- STATISTICS JOBS
- STRIKE JOBS
- THE CHEMICAL ENGINEER
- THE ENGINEER

- → NACE INTERNATIONAL
- → NEDMDG
- → NEW SCIENTIST
- → NEXTPHARMA
- → OILVOICE
- → PHARMA TIMES
- → PHARMATALENTPOOL
- → PHARMIWEB
- → PLANET INTERIM
- → PLANET INTERIM
- → QMED
- → QRCA
- → RENEWABLE ENERGY JOBS
- → RESEARCHJOBFINDER
- → RESPONSE SOURCE
- → THIRD SECTOR
- → WASHINGTON LIFE SCIENCE
- → WASTE JOBS
- → WATER JOBS
- → WIND JOBS
- → WOMEN DIRECTORS
- → WORK ADS
- → WORKANGO
- → XPAIR

Must do's

Simply put, the mindset of a successful audience development professional can best be described as follows:

Relentless

A successful audience development professional will be utterly relentless in their approach to marketing the properties.

Our example business sells subscriptions to professionals working within the industry… and then corporate subscriptions along with marketing services to organisations looking for access to this resident audience.

Never forget this.

Chase Opportunity

The successful audience development professional will always be on the lookout for new web properties, influential/newsworthy people and contacts that might be able to create an advantageous situation for the property, or properties they are promoting.

Create and Optimise Processes

Defining and then creating efficient processes are the mainstay of all audience development activity. Once created ensure that they are relevant and worthwhile. The business does this by monitoring the response rates and resulting 'Bang per Buck'.

For Everything a Reason (FEAR)

The successful professional will take formal notes on all efforts and monitor the results obsessively… which often means daily. This activity will enable the business to 'hack' the methodologies and marketing mix in order to find the best and most successful way forward.

Avoidable Mistakes

Many of the avoidable mistakes listed in this section could be classified as 'smoke and mirrors' and aimed at tricking either auditing businesses, in the case of large scale property portals (for example) into thinking that the audience is greater than it is... or fraudulently overstating the traffic numbers to potential advertisers on blogs and content-based properties.

The following sections of this book highlight mistakes that audience development professionals should be avoid like the plague:

Do Not Buy 404 Redirects, or Domain-based Traffic

Purchasing 404 redirects and/or domain-based traffic used to be common within marketing plans, especially for large-scale e-commerce vendors, who would buy domains based on their historic performance and number of pages indexed within Search Engines.

Upon purchasing the marketer loads the indexed pages with keywords relevant to the domain name and historical link profile in order to ensure SERP's on Google.

However, since the Google Panda update a few years ago, this is not worth the effort. Now those businesses utilising this merely place Google AdWords, or similar on the page, which is (needless to say) against Google AdWords policy.

Likewise, purchasing 404 error pages from established domains is not effective. Some aging but high traffic directories still utilise the strategy of selling redirects off error pages. However, why would a business want to buy an error page?

Do Not Buy Pop-ups, or Pop-unders

Poor marketers will sometimes state that pop-up and pop-under adverts are a low cost way of 'legitimately' boosting traffic to a website. However, it very much depends upon how you define 'legitimate'.

For example, if a publisher, or classifieds website selling advertising was discovered to be boosting its audience numbers by utilising pop-ups and/or pop-under units then it would be disastrous within the marketplace. Depending upon the business model, advertisers would potentially want refunds. Indeed, these ad units are a reputational risk and the units themselves are rarely read.

Also worth noting that a relationship between the pop-up and pop-under units and browser-based toolbars.

Never Buy Fake Traffic

The cheapest form of traffic isn't really traffic at all. It is merely smoke and mirrors. This kind of traffic is produced by large networks who set webpages up with 10-50 frames within them. These 1x1 pixel frames then load in the browser of the visitor, who has no knowledge of the additional websites they are visiting.

This 'trick' is especially prevalent within browser plugins and toolbars and pop-ups with JavaScript disabling the close button for a few seconds as it is easy to magnify the volume of traffic by 10-50 per cent what it actually is.

Today, many toolbars are identified as viruses and Trojans by Anti-virus software.

Again, this highly immoral and can land you in legal difficulties if selling advertising.

Never Buy Likes, Retweets, or Followers

Many organisations and celebrities buy followers on Twitter, Facebook and other social media outlets. This is bad practice and warps your ability to measure the success of the audience development activity.

It is also a false economy as you will get more often than not get ZERO usage out of the purchase.

Do Not Target Poor Quality Links

Low quality links around the web include FFA link sites, most directories, link farms and link networks. Whilst being perfectly legal these links will likely impact your Search Engine rankings in a negative way.

Indeed, it has long been rumoured that unscrupulous Black Hat marketers use FFA links websites to diminish the SERP's of competitors, especially if the competition is extreme.

Steer clear and concentrate on high quality links from relevant sources.

Do Not Overuse your Email Lists

Be careful not to overuse your existing Email lists. Instead limit the usage of each list to the minimum plausible.

Each website and audience has unique qualities (and therefore tolerances) so you in order to limit your Email broadcasts understand the audience and ensure that the message is always as relevant and personalised as possible.

Overusing your list will massively reduce the response rate and annoy potential customers.

Do Not Spam

"Never spam" is an obvious statement to make, however in Australia (especially) it is vital that you have the correct permissions before mailing Email addresses you have acquired from your website, et cetera.

Be especially careful with list swaps and/or list purchases. A business can be crippled by bad PR and legal action from the owners of the Email addresses.

Orgs such as MAPS in the US are quite strict and you can not only lose your Email broadcasting service, but also lose your domain name and server over spam issues.

False Clicks

False clicks is a strategy utilised by many low-end publishers and forums around the world. The way this is done is by setting browsers up on rotating IP addresses (or fake IP's) and then getting a member of staff, or temp to 'test' the website. It rarely works by utilising macros as the user behaviour needs to be different and without obvious pattern, hence a human is required.

This testing requires that the 'tester' opens the browser visits the website from a designated source on a new IP and then browses around the website, including clicking 2-3 banner adverts. The tester then closes his/her browser and deletes cookies, history and more in order to reset the browser for the next visit.

This is the equivalent of fraud... but desperate advertising-driven businesses sometimes do it. Expect this strategy to hit the headlines within the next couple of years.

CHAPTER 11

Commercial Development

So far in this book we have looked at the web sites infrastructure, content audience development activity, sales funnels and functionality.

Now it is time to take a more detailed look at the commercial model for our example business.

The main commercial opportunities are built around paid subscriptions to individual properties within the network.

However, in addition to memberships CPM (cost per thousand) advertising inventory is one of the main commercial activities undertaken on the different properties. Within each grouping are cost structures.

The Business Model

The business publishes and distributes both original and aggregated emerging technology industry content and services using a proprietary, AI-powered digital publishing platform.

The business generates revenue through selling information and marketing-based subscriptions to both organisations and individuals operating within the target industry sectors. Its primary products are:

Individual Subscriptions

An individual subscription consists of access to industry news, jobs listings and career advice, information and associated services aimed at solving problems for professionals working within the sector.

Corporate Subscriptions

Company subscriptions consists of unlimited news and metrics, access to a Deals Database, jobs listings, directory listings and advertising aimed at orgs seeking to reach professionals within industry.

Report Sales

In-house R&A reports are sold via the platform. The report types include Company Profiles, Industry Profiles, Mgmt. Reports and

Marketing Services

Revenue is generated by selling suppliers listings and display advertising. Advertisers will include suppliers to the industry

Quarterly Reviews. 3rd party
reports are sold on the platform.

and those wishing to get their
message in front of the audience.

The Individual Subscription

Individual subscriptions to the portals utilise a 30 day free trial methodology. Once the free period has completed the subscriber is charged at a standard monthly price of $30, with an auto-renewing Quarterly, or Annual contract term.

1x subscriber = $30 per month
5x subscribers = $150 per month
10x subscribers = $300 per month
20x subscribers = $600 per month
50x subscribers = $1,500 per month
75x subscribers = $2,250 per month
100x subscribers = $3,000 per month
250x subscribers = $7,500 per month
500x subscribers = $15,000 per month
1,000x subscribers = $30,000 per month
2,500x subscribers = $75,000 per month
5,000x subscribers = $150,000 per month
7,500x subscribers = $225,000 per month
10,000x subscribers = $300,000 per month

If the payment attempt fails, then further automated attempts to make payment are carried out, as per standard usage terms. If however the payment is declined then the member is notified first by Email and then by telephone in order to motivate them to correct the payment details on the account.

The Corporate Subscription

Corporate subscriptions to the platform are charged based on seats. Each seat has an affordable monthly price of $100, with an auto-renewing annual contract term. This price has been set in order to both maximise the number of seats the larger organisations would purchase; and enable some flexibility in terms of access.

For example, the corporate subscriber could have access to all, or just one individual portal, depending upon requirement.

1x subscriber/seat = $100 per month
5x subscribers/seats = $500 per month
10x subscribers/seats = $1,000 per month
20x subscribers/seats = $2,000 per month
50x subscribers/seats = $5,000 per month
75x subscribers/seats = $7,500 per month
100x subscribers/seats = $10,000 per month
250x subscribers/seats = $25,000 per month
500x subscribers/seats = $50,000 per month
1,000x subscribers/seats = $100,000 per month
2,500x subscribers/seats = $250,000 per month
5,000x subscribers/seats = $500,000 per month

The annual renewal rate for the platform is expected to be between 70-80 per cent, as per industry average for other premium B2B dashboard-based information products.

Marketing Services

The websites will be selling advertising inventory. This inventory will be served and trafficked by the sales team using the OpenX, or DoubleClick DART advertising server.

The following standard advertising units sold are listed below:

Leaderboard Ad

This advert is 728x90 pixels and normally appears at the top of web pages. It achieves a good CTR and as a result is the second highest value advertising unit on the page.

The cost of a Leaderboard should be in the region of $25-30 CPM after reductions on the rate card price.

Medium Rectangles

These adverts are the largest rectangles that appear on the web properties. They are 300x250 pixels and achieve a great CTR. They are the most valuable real estate on the page.

The cost of a medium rectangle should be charged at $35 CPM after reductions on the rate card.

3x Buttons

These 120x90 pixels buttons are placed directly below the menu and are the lowest value positions sold on the site.

The cost of a button should be charged at either a flat rate sponsorship, or charged at a low B2B CPM. $10 CPM would be suitable.

Portal Takeovers

In addition to buying advertising units on the web properties potential advertisers can also buy timed site takeovers. These site takeovers allow the client to change the entire look and feel of the site, or homepage to match their message.

When added to advertising inventory it allows the value of the advertising solution to be substantially increased.

The colours on the homepage and/or site that can be altered include the following:

- → Background
- → Header
- → Menu header
- → Menu background
- → Font colour
- → Footer

The cost of a site takeover to the client would be an additional £1,000 per day. This cost should only ever be accepted if purchased with other inventory across the site.

Supplier Storefronts

Each vertical industry portal will feature a 'Suppliers Directory' of microsites. The easy to browse directory consists of an industry specific taxonomy with businesses listed within the relevant categories.

The MVP for a storefront listing is as follows:

→ Business name
→ Contact name
→ Postal address
→ Recipient Email address
→ Telephone number
→ Homepage, complete with logo and content
→ Company news listings page
→ Company news item page
→ Product listing page
→ Product item page
→ About us page
→ Contact us page
→ Contact us form, complete with free text field at the bottom of every page

This product can be either an annual license subscription-based product, or a single transaction-based product depending upon the set-up and other value-add factors counted in the product specification.

For example, many larger clients on similar commercial products like to include webinar presentations in the bespoke marketing services deal.

The key to the scalability of a microsite-driven business is to have auto-renew on each microsite developed. The microsites are sold via a new business telesales effort at a price-point variable based on the number of categories within the directory the site is linked to; and secondly the size of the business.

The average sale across industry is $3,500 per year, with the minimum acceptable order being $1,500.

Each microsite has feature that company's news and products. In terms of products the arrangement is lead generation in nature, although as a USP sales can be achieved on a transactional basis where a commission on each sale is made along with a listing fee.

This then feeds into news and product-based lists on the site, thus creating free, relevant content for the group. It also enables the sales team to claim that we guarantee coverage of the business on our properties.

Added to the proposition here is one last important feature. A Chatbot. This will drive leads for the client and therefore equate to increased value for the client… and in-turn a superior renewal rate.

Newsletters

Newsletters can be sold by using either the CPM model or a sponsorship model (if number of subscribers is below 10,000).

The average CPM for the newsletters should be $20-25 CPM for either a text advert, or a banner advert within the newsletter.

Three advertising slots should be included in the newsletter enabling the automated newsletter product to achieve a value of between $60-90 CPM.

Email

Commercially, you will likely want to offer some kind of (strictly limited) Email list rentals, as part of the marketing services offering.

Certain business rules will likely be needed with this format of advertising as the business will not want to annoy the membership base.

One way of negating this risk is to not have advertising to paid members. Another way, would be to limit the businesses who will be targeted to those of tangible use to all the members, such as research vendors, events businesses, or recruitment consultants.

Email list rentals will be sold by both in-house advertising sales teams and via 3rd party list brokers across the world.

IN-HOUSE SALES

As a price guide in-house list rentals will generate $300 CPM as a base rate.

Additional costs that will be added include $20 CPM for broadcasting, $25 CPM for additional selects on the database. Additional selects could include, country, sex, job title and industry.

Therefore the average list rental sold in-house should be charged at between $300 and $600 CPM.

3RD PARTY SALES

As a price guide third-party sales achieve between 50 per cent and 60 per cent of the revenue generated by in-house teams. They are therefore used to increase sales.

A list broker in each of the following territories should be sought out:

→ United Kingdom
→ Mainland Europe
→ North America
→ Australia

Upon signing the contract with the list broker pressure should be exerted on the vendor to ensure that they push the list to their clients. List broker's number in the thousands so swapping and changing partner should be considered if the partner fails to make enough sales/revenue per month.

As well as the commercial opportunities already mentioned in this book, other opportunities exist to launch additional newsletter properties based around the magazine subscriber bases.

Micro-Sites

The platform, as outlined in this book enables multiple websites to be built quickly and easily for potential advertising partners.

It is therefore possible to create a bespoke microsite within, or as a standalone for a new vertical, or horizontal.

For example, a microsite could be country-specific, or based around a specific job function such as finance, or technology.

These microsites can include all the normal content types and be sponsored by a business, or organisation that seeks to create and control exposure. The content could be provided either by the business, or by the client, although if it is provided by the client it is worth marking the content as advertorial so as not to damage the overall brand in the eyes of the membership and/or other commercial partners.

Sponsored Webinars

Content could be in the form of recorded Q&A sessions, interviews, presentations, client presentations, seminars, a Breakfast Briefing, online events, et cetera…

The Web seminar could utilize visual content from either video captured, or could include content from a PowerPoint slide pack. An audio commentary would play during playback.

It is normal for Web seminars to be produced by either bespoke in-house software, or (more commonly) by dedicated service providers such as WebEx.

Additionally, supporting content can be loaded to the site in order to increase the value of the offering to the end user.

The sale price for a web seminar with (for example) 200 attendees would be in the region of £10-15,000.

Live Event

The live event model is marketed in a way so that the audience knows the precise time and date the presentation is due to take place. This is often preferred (by lead generation clients) because it means that an agreed number of registered people are participating in real-time.

The audience can ask questions and have the client take part in the general discussion.

After the event has taken place Emails are sent to the registered users and the details passed on to the client.

The event is archived for a set period of time by the service provider.

Sponsorship Model

Once the client has agreed to webinar and the subjects, speakers and timeline has been agreed the following steps will need to be fulfilled:

→ A service provider needs to be sourced
→ Marketing materials and potentially an offer
→ Receive the content from the client
→ A registration form, database and landing page
→ 1x initial Email marketing campaigns to our database
→ 1x Email reminder campaign to the database
→ 1x campaign thanking users for attending
→ The handover of attendees
→ The posting of the event to an archive

Total cost (one-off):
→ $2,000 per event from service provider

Time cost:
→ Preparation of marketing materials = 0.5 days
→ Web development work (form, database and landing pages) = 1 day
→ Email production time = 0.5 days

Podcasts

A daily/weekly podcast should be created with sponsorship sold around it on a CPM model.

In terms of pricing, the average CPM price for a podcast ranges from $18 per 30 second spot to $25 for a 60 second spot. This number will likely be significantly higher for B2B podcasts within high value industry verticals.

Additional Newsletters

The business will launch new newsletters covering the areas where it produces content. By default these areas will be one per sub-site.

Premium Newsletters

Premium newsletters could be created utilizing research and analysis content. The premium newsletter product could sell for between $500-1,000 per year and provide the end user with an ongoing understanding of the trends and issues affecting the industry they work in.

An annual auto-renewal would allow significant revenue growth on this product.

Alternatively, (or additionally) a "free 6-month trial model" could be utilized. Using that option would enable us to generate significant usage and reliance on the product.

Co-branded Newsletters

Clients pay us to produce newsletters based around subject areas they are involved in. This is a form of "conversational marketing" but also has aspects of lead generation. The names of the subscribers are provided to the client.

The offering would consist of two parts:

- ➜ Licensing fee = $15,000 per year
- ➜ Leads generated fee = $7 per subscriber

The potential to gather many thousands of subscribers over the course of a year means that it would potentially be easier to agree the maximum fee with the client at the time of sale.

RSS Feed Advertising

Once the number of readers to the RSS feeds has grown to a level acceptable then it will be possible build an RSS advertising mechanism. This would allow us to automatically insert advertising into the RSS feeds. This simple form would allow the sales team to sell RSS sponsorship packages.

Media Pack and Rate Card

Any successful network of properties selling advertising inventory needs a professional and well thought out media pack.

The media pack and associated rate card will need to be created by either a professional creative agency, or by a skilled in-house creative team using either Quark, or Adobe InDesign. Both PDF and an interactive web format should be available.

The background colour of the media pack should be white as this will increase the odds that the recipient will print it out.

The media pack should include the following:

➜ Clear branding
➜ Overview of the business
➜ Description of properties
➜ Product offering
➜ Demographics and reasons to purchase
➜ Pricing structure
➜ Sales contact details

The media pack should be separate to the rate card price.

Advertising Sales Team

In order to effectively sell advertising inventory a dedicated online advertising sales team will need to be created.

The primary benefit of moving the disparate online sales teams together will be to enable the individual team members to learn from each other.

Team members will then manage their clients and sell using a script.

The earnings and targets for each sales team member are included in the model that relates to this book.

In addition to the earnings, targets and resulting revenues a document outlining the job description for the new position of "Online Advertising Sales Executive" has also been produced.

Online Advertising Sales Executive

Below is the job spec as to be advertised for this position:

We are looking for highly motivated Online Advertising Sales Executives join our team.

Based in our XYZ offices, the successful candidate will be selling high-quality website advertising solutions to both new and existing clients around the world.

PRIMARY RESPONSIBILITIES:

➜ Managing personal call rates
➜ Defining most relevant solution to respective client
➜ Relationship and account building
➜ Making proposals
➜ Ensuring that the proposals and solution is understood
➜ Closing the sale
➜ Generating repeat business
➜ Measurement and reporting of results to client

Required Experience and Skills:

➜ At least one year of experience in selling advertising-based solutions

→ Understanding of the internet and Email as a communications medium

→ Experience of working with potential advertisers to remove their objections

→ Experience of managing the sales lifecycle.

→ Understanding of measurement and metrics

→ Excellent communication skills

→ Degree, or additional related experience

PERSONAL CHARACTERISTICS:

INNOVATIVE: Candidate should be able to think outside the box to find the optimal solution to match advertiser requirements to available solution(s).

DESIRE: Candidate will have a passion for selling and be driven to succeed.

WORK ETHIC: Candidate can reject setbacks and enthusiastically persists until goals are achieved.

COMMUNICATION: Candidate will be a natural communicator with people from all walks of life.

ACCOUNTABILITY: Candidate should be a results-oriented team player who leads by example and holds themselves accountable.

LEARNING: Candidate should have a desire to learn about the company, the products/services and solutions.

COMMITMENT: Candidate will show commitment to the task and be willing to go that extra yard in order to succeed.

UNDERSTANDING: Candidate should have an understanding of the media business and the marketing of content.

R&A Report Pricing Structure

Single-copy R&A report products will be available for immediate online download across the network of portals.

Based on prices for similar products from vendors such as Datamonitor, Hoovers and GlobalData the following price points will be attractive:

→ **COMPANY PROFILES, INCLUDING SWOTS** – Priced at $100 each

→ **INDUSTRY PROFILES** – Priced at $250 each

→ **MANAGEMENT REPORTS** – Priced at $850 each

→ **MONTHLY REVIEWS** – Priced at $50 each

→ **QUARTERLY REVIEWS** – Priced at $100 each

→ **ANNUAL REVIEWS** – Priced at $300 each

In addition to the reports branded with the company name, other research reports from 3rd party vendors will be made available for sale through the portals.

Typically, these reports will be sold on a 50:50 revenue share basis, with the sale being completed on the relevant portal, therefore all revenues collected. Reports will then be delivered by the partner and the business then invoiced.

CHAPTER 12

Understanding the Membership Economy

I n 2015 Robbie Kellman Baxter released her seminal book, called 'The Membership Economy: Find Your Super Users, Master the Forever Transaction, and Build Recurring Revenue' and along the way coined the definitive phrase, 'The Membership Economy'.

Whilst my own methodologies, as highlighted in this book sometimes differ from Robbie's I would thoroughly recommend purchasing that book as it offers readers a considerable background and detail into best practice methodologies and more.

By offering both individual and corporate subscriptions our example portal business operates within the membership economy.

Indeed, the subscription model is the backbone of our example portal business. It is therefore vitally important that the business gets the subscription model right and understands the drivers and key attributes of operating a successful business within the membership economy.

Maximising the Customer Lifetime Value

In order to achieve the best growth levels possible, it is important to maximise the Customer Lifetime Value. This is best achieved by motivating usage and retaining the paying subscriber at the maximum value for as long as possible.

Another method of achieving an increased Customer Lifetime Value is by value-adding to a reduced subscription, or speeding up the renewal timeframe.

Membership Models

Whilst there is a certain degree of overlap between the various membership models, below is a list of the seven types of membership website you are likely to see as you sojourn around the web:

Full Access

This type of membership site allows users to access absolutely everything straight away. The model normally utilises a longer-term subscription plan (annual, or quarterly) and offers additional value to users to ensure that the churn rate is controlled.

One example here is a GlobalData subscription which offers access to everything within the vertical, but the minimum subscription being for 12 months.

Drip Fed

This kind of membership site involves a monthly payment for access to a private area with new content added on a regular basis, hence the term 'drip feed'.

An example of this kind of property is Business Insider, who enable users to pay a monthly subscription to access hard to find data, which is added to the property monthly.

Fixed Term

The trend within online education is to offer courses on a membership basis, behind a secure paywall. The courses themselves are normally timed and modular in nature, thus ensuring a low churn rate.

The commercial model for courses, are normally based around a fixed fee, but can be paid for in regular instalments.

The Open University in the UK is an example of this kind of membership model.

Community-based

Social websites are becoming more and more popular, and are easy to create with the proliferation of membership, group and forum plugins out there on platforms such as Joomla and WordPress.

With this model the website charges its user a monthly fee for access to private specific areas of the property, such as group-based content, or messaging-based functionality. The user only has access to that specific portion of the property for as long as they pay.

Service-based

This type of membership model is based on the access and delivery of a service. Most SaaS businesses utilise this model.

One example of a service-based membership model would be SalesForce.com

Product-based

This type of model consists of a digital product being delivered via a membership site, as either a password protected download, or via a defined access area on the platform. The commercial model is normally a one-time fee for access to an individual item.

An example of this product is Dunn and Bradstreet who enable you to buy access to a single report; and then attempt to upsell you to more reports post joining.

Hybrid

I have left this model to last as it is (as the name suggests) a hybrid mix of the options above.

This books example portal business utilises a hybrid model, borrowing aspects from 2-3 of these disparate models.

Choosing the Correct Model

Personally, I think about membership models by breaking down the following attributes:

The Offering

The content and/or functional offering available on the portal. The various options for this are:

PREMIUM CONTENT – This includes everything from single-copy R&A reports, through to high value data sets.

NETWORKING – Community-based discussion, focus groups, forums and more.

LIBRARY – This consists of the majority of the content offering, arranged into silos, such as jobs, news items and more.

PRODUCT – This would include core functionality as well as content sets such as survey data, polls, white papers, non-premium company profiles and printable files available via download.

SERVICE – This could include everything from webinars, eLearning advice and consulting through to SaaS social analytics services and more.

The Delivery

This portion of the model is all about how the product is delivered to the members. Most editorial-based products utilise both these methodologies, so it is not necessarily an either/or.

DRIP-FED – This methodology involves gradually releasing content and/or functionality over the set period of the subscription.

INSTANT – The subscriber gains immediate access to the product.

The Access

This portion of the model dictates what kind of access privileges each individual, or corporate member given:

LIFETIME – This is where you offer your subscribers a lifetime access to the offering upon subscription.

PAYG – This option is based around the member purchasing access as and when needed. For example, you might charge a membership fee for access privileges, but a separate fee to access certain content types.

FIXED-TERM – This is where the subscription runs for a stated period. Quarterly, or annual subscriptions are amongst the month commonly used periods for the subscription. Once the period ends, then access also ends.

RECURRING – The access level is based around immediate and continual for as long as you keep paying the rolling subscription. Traditional tech platforms such as web site hosting operates using this kind of model.

Onboarding

As with most subscription-based businesses, without oodles of cash to spend on marketing attaining membership hyper-growth organically is key.

This is a simple visualisation of the business that best displays how to achieve membership hyper-growth:

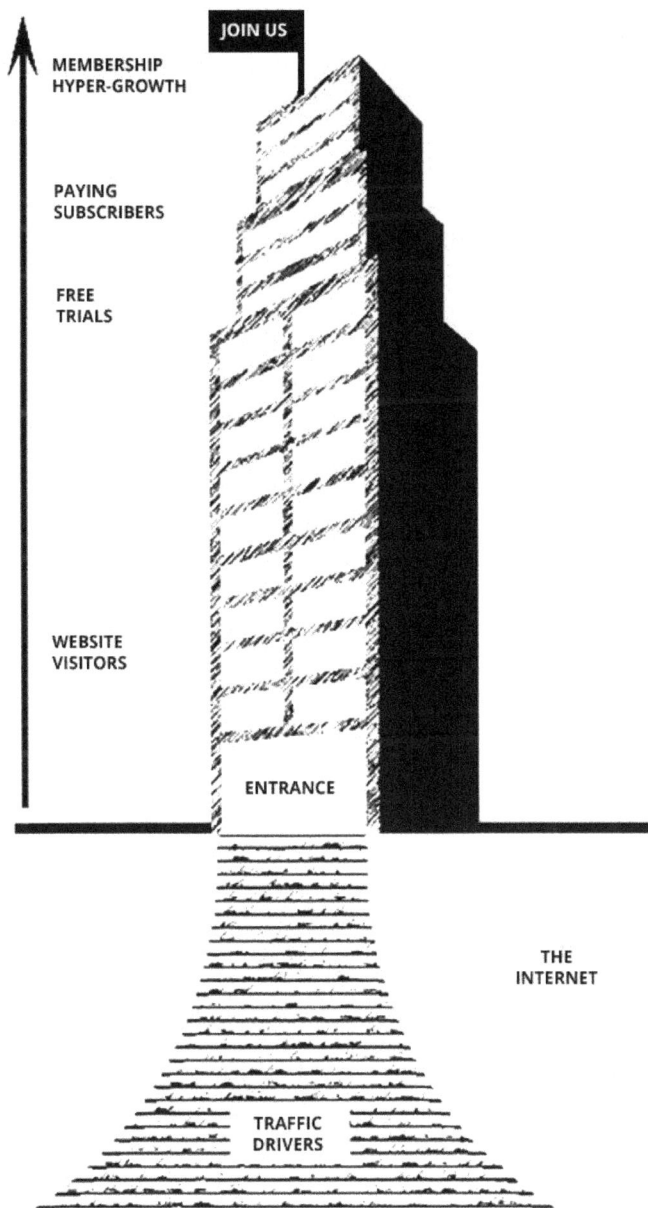

JOIN US

MEMBERSHIP
HYPER-GROWTH

PAYING
SUBSCRIBERS

FREE
TRIALS

WEBSITE
VISITORS

ENTRANCE

THE
INTERNET

TRAFFIC
DRIVERS

The aim is to get the potential users from the roadside, into the lift and up to the top floor where they will encourage others within their networks to join on your behalf.

A brief explainer is as follows:

TRAFFIC SOURCES – Traffic is sourced from the internet. This constitutes the entirety of audience development activity.

WEBSITE VISITORS – Once the audience is acquired then this becomes about retention and conversion of the visitor into either a free trial user, or paying member. This is achieved by encouraging each step of the process and removing any objections.

FREE TRIALS – Once the user has hit the usage limit of the free access then they are offered a free trial for a stipulated amount of time. Reminders counting down the usage are sent via Email every couple of days. If the user stops using the website during this time then prompts are sent instead. Remember, you want the user using.

PAYING SUBSCRIPTION – Because the user is using the property… and they have already entered payment information then they deem the membership valuable. They then become a subscriber.

MEMBERSHIP HYPER-GROWTH – Once the subscribed the business needs to motivate the user to advertise the business for you. They do this by (1) submitting their Email address book; (2) receiving discounts/offers; (3) more…

Membership Retention

One of the keys to success in building a membership business is having a healthy retention rate. I gauge this as above 75 per cent.

Below is a list of things you can do to maximise the member retention numbers for our example portals:

FACE TO FACE MEET-UPS – I believe it is important to put a face on the business. Arranging bi-monthly meet-ups with members either at the office, or at a different venue is a great method of engagement and installs a sense of community and (importantly) additional value to the subscription.

MONTHLY CALLS – Have the editorial team do regular (for example) monthly calls to members. This could be to discuss the latest happenings within the industry, or for some other reason. –The key thing to remember is to keep everything on topic.

QUICK WINS – Add more 'quick win' content and/or functionality to the property. This book features many such ideas and it is about prioritising them and running with what you think will work best. –I think of it as 'low hanging fruit'.

BE A VOICE – Become the voice for professionals working within your space. During my time career within publishing I have always sought for the platform I am managing to become the voice on the industry the business will become vital to professionals working within the sector.

OFFER LEADERSHIP – One way of becoming the voice of the industry is by offering leadership based on the issues; dominating the coverage; and being the centre for debate. The Contributor Payment

Model discussed in detail in this book will potentially help you here.

RELEVANCE – In terms of membership retention, it is vital that the business concentrates on offering its users relevant products and services. –It is sometimes wise to think outside of the box and brainstorm ideas. Ask yourself, what would a professional cameraman want to know? What would a set designer like to read? Et cetera, et cetera, et cetera.

DIRECTION – Provide your membership with a homepage. A place where they can jump in and out.

For example, if the website is jobs-based, why offer a homepage to registered members that is dominated by news… and effectively looks the same as for non-subscribers. This immediately devalues the entire proposition in the eyes of the paying subscriber.

REGULAR SURVEYS – Conduct a regular survey of existing members to better understand usage patterns and requirements.

DOWNSELL – Provide a 'Downsell' option. This could be a slimmed down version of the subscription, or product/service offering for those that want out.

Do some internal research and set triggers in the CMS once a member has unsubscribed with the chosen option, based on usage pattern of the subscriber. Considerable number of opportunities and possibilities here when utilising a metered subscription model.

➜ **EXAMPLE 1** –The person unsubscribing only views jobs. They now have a job. –Offer them a news-based subscription for $$$

➜ **EXAMPLE 2** – The person is unemployed and cannot afford the subscription. –Offer them access to jobs for $$$

CONTENT DIARY - Create a content calendar so that members know what is coming up. –This also motivates usage.

DAILY VIDEO – This works because it humanises the business.

CULT OF PERSONALITY – The 'Cult of Personality' has been around forever, but the theory behind it was mastered by old Stalinist and Marxist leaders in the Soviet-era in order to control the population by controlling thought leaders and the method of communication. Nikita Khrushchev was perhaps the key proponent of this. It works when people conflate an issue with a message and a persons' personality.

CONTENT SERIES – Add series-based content to the property. This means the membership know what to expect. Newspapers do this effectively by offering serialised versions of novels/autobiographies.

BE VITAL – Provide software, templates or tools to your members that they would miss if they left.

For example, it might be worth looking at acquiring some templated business-oriented letters.

ADD INTERACTIVITY – The addition of relevant interactivity to any membership-based property automatically motivates and increases usage. Increasing usage on the property will in-turn lead to a better renewal rate.

TESTIMONIALS – Grab testimonials from users relating to finding a job, solving a problem, et cetera. Getting quotes is especially powerful for both selling new subscriptions… and just as importantly reinforcing the power of the proposition to subscribers who perhaps are thinking about not renewing.

THIRD PARTY VALUE-ADD's – Look to value add products and services from third parties and notify the membership monthly as to new offers. These are benefits. They are reasons to stay subscribed.

FOLLOW-UP EMAILS – Once the user has joined the website, ensure that they can get started and know how to get the best out of a subscription. If they have not used the website in the time post sign-up session then automagically send them an Email 4-5 working days later telling them how to get started.

This is to ensure usage and remind those potentially on a free trial that the subscription exists.

FAILED BILLING – This functionality is important because it sends automated follow-ups for failed payments via the payment gateway, as per legal rights.

USER NOTIFICATIONS – Ensure that users know how to use the website and know when any significant changes and/or content sets are added. –It's all about reinforcing the community.

AVERAGE TENURE – Work out what the average tenure of a member is and then react in terms of incentives/value offering, et cetera. It is vital to be on the front foot.

BONUSES – Incentivise members to commit to longer subscriptions. This is especially valid when the business is looking to put the price of a subscription up.

VIDEO MESSAGE - Add an auto-play personal video from the face of the business (management, or Editor) to the cancellation page. This will put a face next to the business. Folk are less keen to cancel products/services when they associate a real person to said product/service.

EXIT SURVEY – This short 5-6 question automated survey includes an offer and enables you to better understand the reasoning why the person has left.

Once the results are in, then the recipient can be automagically sent an offer negating the reasons for unsubscribing.

MAXIMISE CONTENT – Break each content item down. Slice and Dice. This doc includes a ton of information on this methodology. This is key to building a scalable content business.

OFFER VIDEO – Offer regular videos to members. More and more people are turning to video as the primary way of consuming information.

CHATBOT – Many Chatbot services exist. More information on the implementation of this functionality can be found elsewhere in this book.

CERTIFICATION – This is a complicated subject and more research would be needed, but if you were to partner with an eLearning provider; software provider such as Google, or Microsoft; or offline educational establishment then certification and training could be a great 'low hanging fruit' addition to the proposition.

THREADED FORUMS – These allow conversations to take place between members, but controlled by either a taxonomy, or folksonomy (depending upon model). –Conversation equals value.

GAMIFICATION – Implement gamification or progress tracking for content on the site, in the form of Badges, rankings, et alia.

Works especially well with training sessions and eLearning modules, but in theory could be used right the way across the property. Reddit is a great example of a membership platform utilising badges.

EDIT PROFILES – Allow users/members to update payment profiles, name, Email address, et cetera easily. This will save time and trouble that always costs the business money.

CASE STUDIES – Feature case studies on the site in order to reinforce the value of the offering and how the business solved XYZ problem.

Future Opportunities

The example business we have used in this example is massively scalable both in terms of the industry verticals and horizontals it can operate in; and also in terms of the commercialisation of the proprietary technology developed.

As with all businesses, if you can get the initial business model right then you have a basis from which to expand.

Some of the best advice ever given to me from an old boss was, once you see success then accelerate, innovate and dominate the space you want to operate in.

Additional Industry Verticals

The business, by its very nature is designed to expand into new industry verticals as and when resources allow. The scalability of the technology platform and speed in which new industry vertical websites can be launched positions the business exceptionally well to potentially dominate any new industry vertical.

For example, the business could be replicated across any/all the industry verticals below. The only limiting factors are the content production cost; and specific viability of each sector.

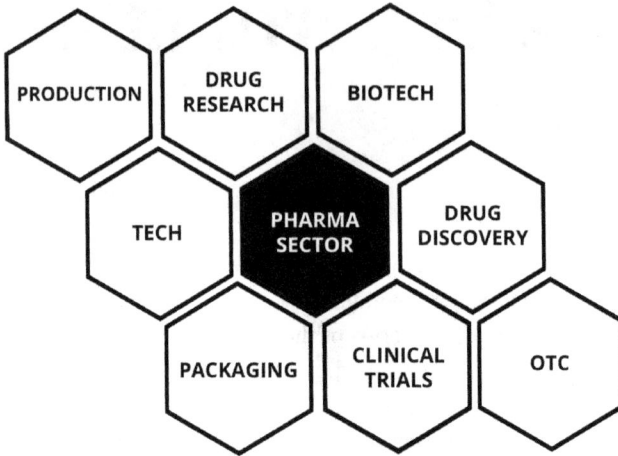

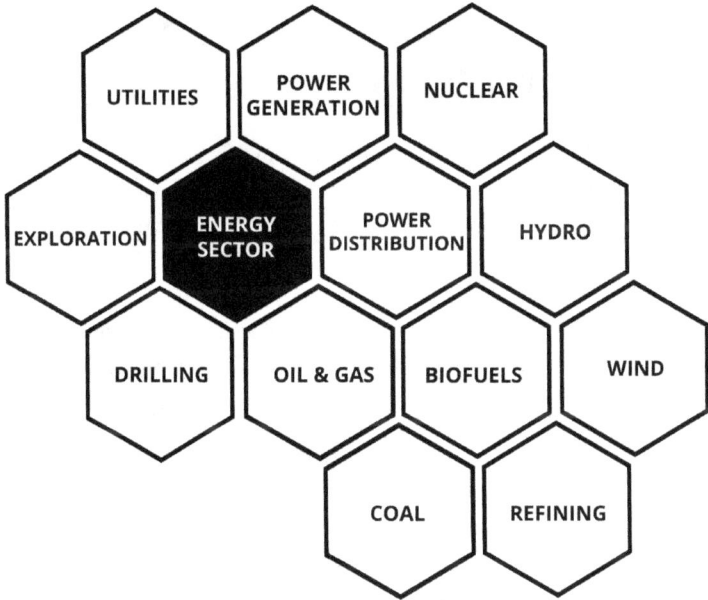

Technology Licensing

As a technology platform, the business outlined in this book has the unique opportunity to license its proprietary technology to not only market research and industry analysis providers, but also to most publishing companies.

The way that the consumer absorbs content is fundamentally changing. The platform would place the business in an extraordinary position to capitalise on this fundamental change.

Premium Content

The market research and industry analysis industry has revenues in excess of $30 billion (USD) per year, with key players including IMS, Gartner, Forrester, Informa, GlobalData, polling businesses, analytics companies and contract research vendors.

Additional premium content could be sourced from relevant research report suppliers across the world.

The company would be able to use its membership to market these reports on behalf of the external provider. Normal revenue share percentages are 60:40 towards the content author.

For example, a few years ago the average price of premium research reports at one leading vendor was $3,500, which would equate to $1,400 profit per report sold, but $3,500 towards the revenue figure as the business will be performing the transaction and passing the order over to the partner for completion. This is the most transparent way of selling reports.

As a premium content provider, the business has the opportunity to license its in-house content to 3rd parties by syndication and/or via another licensing model.

Content Licensing and Distribution

Because of the content types and volume of content produced by the business, it can be cut up into relevant sections and content types and then licensed to service and information providers.

Generally-speaking, the value of content licensing and distribution is dependent upon the industry, type and nature of the content produced. Licensing premium information can generate many millions of Dollars a year. Licensing news content is worth considerably less.

Single-copy sales via 3rd party websites is hugely profitable and can vastly increase the number of sales made. Both licensing and using 3rd party businesses to sell reports are crucial to all premium content producers.

Outlets and opportunities for new sales channels include the following sources.

SINGLE COPY SALES	LICENSED DISTRIBUTION
→ MarketResearch.com	→ Factiva
→ Hoovers (DnB)	→ EBSCO
→ Research & Markets	→ Thomson Gale
→ Global Markets Direct	→ Intranets and Extranets
→ Thomson Gale	

Conferences and Events

Additionally, the focused network aspect of the portals open up for a global B2B conferences and events-based business to be shaped around industry news, analysis and prognostications.

To begin with a specialist events and conferencing business could be sought in order to partner with.

Alternatively, a research vendor covering the same, or related space could be a great source for additional content and relevance.

Vertical Advertising Network

A vertical advertising network could eventually be created. This advertising sales network will sell the inventory of web properties both internally within the group and also with external sites within the same (or similar) space, or based on demographic makeup.

This approach would enable the business to (1) sell out its inventory; (2) increase the value of the advertising revenue generated; and (3) sell inventory across different properties.

In terms of external partners, the business would operate on a revenue share.

Most inventory (by volume) is sold via advertising agencies, although the platform would also feature an e-commerce enabled facility whereby website users can book, pay and monitor campaigns online.

Additionally, a small new business sales team would be created to generate this additional business.

CHAPTER 14

Key Take Homes

T his book discusses a lot of new developments and methodologies within the publishing space. Whilst writing it, in order to foster massively accelerated growth, I have concentrated on outlining the specific things that I believe will work the best for the example business.

I would highlight the following as the key take homes from this book:

Contributor Payment Model

A truly meritocratic editorial model that enables improved flexibility and scalability for the business.

The Metered Paywall

Move the business to a Metered Paywall model, whilst still offering a free trial. This will enable the business to better market itself in a multitude of ways, including search, social media and job Search Engines such as Broadbean, Indeed, Simply Hired and the myriad of others.

Audience

Without an audience you do not have a business. Again, look not only at the current business, but also at the UK and the new synergistic verticals.

Membership Hyper-growth

Develop your sales funnel in order to maximise the potential of achieving membership hyper-growth. To do this you need to utilise the power of the network, not marketing spend.

Audience Development Manager

If you are managing the marketing internally, you should hire a decent Marketing Manager to both manage audience and subscription drives, but also business development activities.

Do not waste your time with anybody under $120k (all in). From experience, they are not competitive in the marketplace and a false economy.

Sales Funnel Optimisation

As a fundamental part to all sales and marketing efforts, the sales funnel needs to be continually tailored and optimized to yield the best possible returns.

With the free report, the free trial AND the Metered Paywall you have a good opportunity to optimise the entire process.

Platform Development

Any platform-based business needs to ensure that it has significant unique IP both in terms of content and in terms of proprietary technology. As a result, utilising progressive product development strategies all products need to become more substantial.

The example business we have created in this book achieves this by integrating certain AI-based features in a unique way; and developing significant content IP.

Embrace Video Content

Usage patterns have changed utterly in the past 5-6 years. Video is now the prime method for developing truly immersive, high value content, even in B2B. Content remains King.

Product Innovation

As mentioned in the Platform Development point, AI and other new technologies are not just nice to haves, but also will be expected by end users over the coming few years.

The next generation of platform will utilise not just artificial intelligence in the back-end, but also with new user interfaces and immediacy.

Plan for this.

Model it

When developing either a new product, business unit, or business my approach has always been one of modelling it beforehand. As a stakeholder you need to understand what the business is, how it operates and what the final destination is. You can do all of this within the kind of business model I have outlined in this book.

CHAPTER 15

Glossary of Terms

The terms included in this section may be used at times within the book, so have therefore been explained and defined for greater clarity and understanding:

A/B TESTING – A controlled experiment with two variants.

A/B/C TESTING – Same as A/B testing, but using a third variant.

ABOVE THE FOLD – The part of the page you can see without scrolling down or over.

ACTIVEX – A technology introduced by Microsoft in the mid 1990's. It provides a simple way for software developers to add functionality and interface with software installed on your computer.

AD EXTENSIONS – Added information that is included in your text ad.

ADCENTER – Bing Ads powers paid search results on Microsoft's Bing.

ADVERTORIAL – An advert that is deliberately styled to look like the editorial of a newspaper, magazine, or web publication. The television equivalent is an infomercial.

ADVOCACY JOURNALISM – This is a genre of journalism that intentionally and transparently adopts a non-objective viewpoint, usually in order to play to its target audience, or potential audience.

AIDA – This standard for 'Attention, Interest, Desire, Action'.

AMA – Ask me anything. A new type of open interview pioneered on Reddit, but now found across social media and the various video platforms.

ARPA – Average Revenue per advertiser.

ARPU – This is simply the average revenue per user.

ARTIFICIAL INTELLIGENCE – AI is an intelligence displayed by computers, in contrast with the organic/natural intelligence displayed by humans and other sentient animals.

ASPECT RATIO – This is the relationship between the width and the height of your video dimensions expressed as a ratio.

ASTROTURFING – This is a term used to describe fake grassroots support on websites and/or blog comments. This is a method frequently (and effectively) employed by public relations agencies, political groups and the advertising industry.

ATL MARKETING – This means 'above the line' marketing, which includes marketing activities aimed at reaching the widest possible number of people. As a result it is largely untargeted and of less relevance to small scale businesses.

An example of an ATL marketing campaign would be a national television, or radio advert.

AUDIENCE DEVELOPMENT – This includes absolutely everything to do with the generation of an audience; the increase in usage and/or conversions by that audience; and the measurement of the audience.

AUTOCUE – Sometimes called a teleprompter. This is a platform that enables presenters and newsreaders to follow a pre-written script.

AUTOMAGICAL – To complete a technology-related task in a seemingly ingenious, automatic way.

AVERAGE DAILY GROWTH – Average rate at which you add subscribers.

AVERAGE SUBSCRIPTION – Average number of days active for a subscriber.

BACKLINKS – Links from other websites pointing to any particular page on your site.

BEACONS – A form of tech that allows marketers to connect and engage wirelessly with consumers via their mobile devices.

BELOW THE FOLD – The part of the page hidden when first viewed in the browser.

BOT – A software application that runs automated tasks. Sometimes called a Robot.

BOTTOM THIRD EFFECTS – These are graphical effects added to a video in the bottom third of the screen, such as the name of the presenter, et cetera.

BT – Behavioural targeting.

BTL MARKETING – This means 'below the line' marketing, which includes very specific and targeting marketing activities.

For example, a PPC campaign on google AdWords would be BTL as it is highly targeted and specific to a select group of potential customers.

BUYER PERSONA – A fictional depiction of your target customers, based on knowns plus assumptions.

BYLINE – The name of the author of a specific content item. Within the news publishing business, it t is always best to have a named name rather than a 'staff writer' as google (for example) will not feature your content on its newsfeed without the authors name.

CANONICAL TAG – A tag that tells Google, et al which page is preferred when two URLs are duplicate, or dangerously similar.

CDP – Content delivery platform.

CHATBOT – This is software which conducts a conversation via auditory or textual methods, often mimicking a human.

CHROMAKEY – this is a colour background, normally either a green screen, or blue screen, but also potentially white, or black. They are used to standardise the background and remove any shadows to enable any and all special effects to be added.

To add the effects, all you need to do is isolate and mask the specific colour and replace with whatever you want. This is how virtual newsrooms are built.

CHURN RATE – Annualised rate at which customers cancel their subscriptions.

CHURNALISM – This equates to bad journalism, where the writer merely churns out rewrites of press releases. –To be frank, much journalism today consists of this.

CMS – Content management system.

COCA – On an individual scale, this is the total 'cost of customer acquisition' (CoCa).

COHORT – A related segment or group within an audience.

COMPOSITING – This is the process of combining multiple images using post production software.

CONTEXTUAL ADVERTISING – This is used in display advertising networks and on Search Engines where advertising is placed automagically next to relevant content.

CPC – this stands for 'cost per click' and is the unit of measurement when calculating the cost of each click in a PPC campaign

CPL – Cost Per Lead.

CPM – Cost Per Mille.

CTR – Click through rate.

CUSTOMER LIFETIME VALUE – The average value of each member on the portal. In terms of formulating the calculation, assume that if the individual subscription price is $100 per month and the member is a paying full tariff subscriber for 12 months, then the resulting Customer

Lifetime Value is $1,200.

DEEP LINK RATIO – Most mature content-based websites have a natural link profiles. As you do SEO activity, it is vitally important to keep the ratio near natural levels.

For example, do not merely send every link to the homepage, or other list pages... that is what is known as over optimisation and is (genuinely) terrible for the search engine performance of a website.

DEEP LINKING – Linking to a page other than the homepage.

DOWDIFICATION – A deliberate omission of a term, or terms in order to change the meaning of a quote. The name refers to the controversial journalist Maureen Dowd. Many politically-biased publications do this each and every day... again in order to play to the audience.

DIY – Relates to web development and means 'don't repeat yourself'.

DYNAMIC RETARGETING – Adverts shown to users who have already visited the site. They often contain images and information about the exact item they viewed.

ECPM – This stands for effective CPM (cost per mille).

EDGERANK – This is the name of the algorithm Facebook uses to rank pages, groups, or individual accounts to determine which posts from those accounts will appear in the feed.

ELEMENTS / OVERLAYS – This is a video effect added to a video.

ENDOTHERMIC – Absorbing.

ENTERPRISE SEARCH – Professional quality search capability aimed at Enterprises. The core functionality often includes facetted search, advanced functionality to tailor relevance and results on your server; and bespoke business rules.

For example, the excellent open source enterprise Search Engines Apache SOLR, or Sphinx.

EVOLUTIONARY ECONOMICS - Evolutionary economics is a mainstream economic theory dealing with the study of processes that transform organisations, industries and entire economies using evolutionary game theory and the biological evolutionary methodology developed by Charles Darwin.

EXOTHERMIC – Releasing.

FPS – In video, this means Frames per second. –In order to produce good quality video with no missed frames you will want to produce video with a minimum of 24-25 FPS, which is what most movies use.

FREEMIUM – A free service with the option for customers to upgrade to a paid, premium version.

GEO-BLOCKING – This is where online content providers limit access based on your geographic location.

GONZO JOURNALISM – This is a type of journalism where the story is written without any claims of objectivity… and often includes the writer as part of the story. YouTube is one of the primary sources for Gonzo Journalism.

GROK – A Swedish word that means to by intuition, or by empathy entirely understand the issue/subject/..

GUI – Graphical user interface.

HARD BOUNCE – When an Email bounces back to the broadcaster because the Email address does not exist, or refuses to receive Emails from the broadcaster.

HEATMAP – A graphical representation of data that uses a system of color-coding to represent different value.

HYPER LOCAL – A term used in journalism to refer to content written and/or read by residents within a defined, small scale geographic area (e.g. Kingston, or Brighton in Melbourne).

IFRAME – This is short for inline frame. This is a HTML element that allows an external webpage, or ad unit to be displayed on a page.

INVERTED PYRAMID – This is perhaps the most common method of writing news content. This structure is frequently used by journalists in writing news stories… and it involves arranging the information of a news story in descending order, by importance.

This (quite literally) means that the most important or newsworthy aspects of the story come first. –This is reinforced by SEO 101 techniques, which generally require the most relevant content to appear at the top of the article.

KANO MODEL – Kano is a product development theory that classifies features into five simple areas to aid prioritisation.

LATENCY – In computing the word latency describes some kind of delay, often caused by lack of system resources either on the network side, or on the client side.

LEADERBOARD – Ad unit that is 728x90 pixels.

LEADIN – Introduction to a recorded/filmed excerpt from a news source, or another journalist.

LEAD MAGNET – This is a (hopefully) irresistible offer the marketer puts together for visitors who in exchange for offering their contact information will gain access to the product. The goal of the Lead Magnet is to increase the number of relevant leads within the sales funnel.

LEAN-TESTING – Refers to the process of testing assumptions, whilst managing costs effectively.

LEARNABILITY – This term describes a platforms capability to help users become familiar with the functionality easily, speedily and with efficiency.

LONG TAIL PUBLISHERS – Normally blogs that are supported by programmatic networks, or similar and based around keywords.

MACHINE LEARNING – Machine learning (ML) is a field within computer science that gives computers the ability to learn without being explicitly programmed.

MERCHANT ACCOUNT – This is a type of bank account that allows a business to accept credit card (and often) debit card transactions.

METERED PAYWALL – Simply put, this is a type of paywall that enables non-members to view a stated number of pages over a stated number of days.

MULTIVARIATE TESTING – Same as A/B testing, but with many variants.

MVP – Minimum viable product.

NARROWCASTING – Disseminate information and content to a localised, or specialised audience.

NPD – New product development.

OCCAM'S RAZOR – This is a problem-solving principle attributed to William of Ockham in the 14th century which equates to the simplest explanation being more likely to be accurate than more complicated explanations.

OFF PAGE SEO – Generically, this includes all optimisation activities 'offsite' such as link building, directory submissions and bookmarking.

ON PAGE SEO – This is search engine optimisation activity that takes place on the website itself.

On-page SEO includes everything from metatags and code optimisation through to sitemap generation and page load speed. However, by far the most important aspect of on page SEO is the optimisation of the content item and homepage for relevant keywords.

This is especially important for e-commerce and/or publishing websites.

PARALLELISM – The presentation of ideas in similar grammatical or visual forms.

PERIOD CHURNED CUSTOMER – Number of customers lost during a specific period.

PING - This means "to get the attention of" or "to check for the presence of" another party online.

PODCASTING – This is an audio-only version of a blog

PPC – This stands for pay per click, which is the standard format of advertising used on google and Facebook.

PRE-ROLL – A promotion, or advert that plays before the content. This is the most common form of advertising on YouTube.

PROGRAMMATIC ADVERTISING – This simply refers to advertising that is purchased/sold/delivered using automation.

PUSH NOTIFICATIONS – These are messages that pop up on mobile devices and some browsers. An important part of app marketing.

REBILLING STRATEGY – The practice of renewing active subscribers on a set timetable.

RESPONSIVE DESIGN – this means the webpage notes what browser and resolution the visitor is using and then offers the best width and user experience the design has to offer. This is increasingly important because mobile and small screen usage via tablets are becoming more and more prevalent. It is imperative that all new web properties have a responsive platform.

RIFF – Often an enthusiastic, detail-driven opinion piece.

RON – Run of network adverts.

ROS – Run of site adverts.

RSS – a format of xml called really simple syndication, or rich site summary depending on your era. It remains the format of xml most commonly used to syndicate and deliver regularly updating content, such as news, blogs and simple data sets such as share price data.

SAAS – Software as a Service

SANDBOXING – This is where a developer isolates applications.

SDE – Seller discretionary earnings. This is a method of enterprise valuation used for smaller digital properties. It's a calculation based on 'Revenue – Cost of Goods Sold – OPEX + Owner Compensation.

SEF – Search engine friendly.

SERP'S – This stands for search engine results page. The page searchers see after they've entered their query into the search box. This page lists several web pages related to the searcher's query, sorted by search relevance.

SLICE AND DICE – The strategy of cutting an original piece of content up and/or joining it together with other content items in order to create a new content item.

SOCIAL GRAPH – The mapping of connections between individuals through one, two, or potentially many social platforms.

SOCIAL PRESENCE – Activity on social media.

SOFT BOUNCE – When an Email bounces back to the broadcast software due to a temporary problem such as the recipients' inbox being full.

SOV – Share of voice relates to the percentage share of available advertising inventory.

SSL CERTIFICATE – this stands for 'secure socket layer' and is the certificate that identifies the owner of the server to the users' browser. Without an up-to-date one, modern browsers will show a warning whenever the visitor lands on https://...

STRUCTURED SNIPPETS – Allow your advert to highlight specific aspects of the product. Great for displaying value, or the proposition.

SUBSCRIPTION FLOW – Also known as 'Subscribe Flow'. The steps by which customers become subscribers.

THREE POINT LIGHTING – This is the most common lighting setup. It lights a subject from three different sources in order to control shadows and balance contrast.

TRIPWIRE MARKETING – This is the methodology used to turn a lead into a paying subscriber by making them a simple, low-cost offer for a related product. Once they are within the sales funnel the marketer then has the opportunity to upsell them to the desired product.

TTL MARKETING – this mean 'through the line' marketing, which equates to a mixture of both ATL and BTL marketing activity.

UI – User interface.

UVP – Unique value proposition.

VLOGGING – This is simply the video version of a blog.

VOD – Video on demand.

VORTAL – A term to describe a vertical industry portal.

WYSIWYG – Within editing, what you see is what you get.

YIELD PER VISIT – The average revenue generated by each visit

Index

ABOUT THE AUTHOR

Robert J Phillips has 15+ years leadership experience at CEO and Executive-level.

The digital businesses and/or products envisaged, developed, delivered and then managed have generated more than $130 million in profit, with exceptional margins for a variety of large >$2 Billion media conglomerates listed on the LSE and exciting start-up, or early-stage companies in London, San Francisco and Melbourne.